THE DETROIT LIONS

An Illustrated Timeline

The Lions miss a field goal in the championship against the Cleveland Browns on December 29, 1957 in Detroit.
COURTESY OF GETTY IMAGES

THE DETROIT LIONS

An Illustrated Timeline

BY DAVE BIRKETT

REEDY PRESS

Reedy Press
PO Box 5131
St. Louis, MO 63139, USA
www.reedypress.com

Library of Congress Control Number: 2024939006

ISBN: 9781681065472

Cover and Interior Design: Eric Marquard

All front cover images courtesy of Getty Images. All back cover images courtesy of Getty Images.

All interior photos courtesy of Getty Images unless otherwise noted.

Printed in Canada
25 26 27 28 5 4 3

DEDICATION

To Avery and Jack, nothing beats being your dad. Work hard, be kind, enjoy life.

The Lions take the field before a game against the Minnesota Vikings at Ford Field on January 7, 2024.
COURTESY OF GETTY IMAGES

CONTENTS

A team photo of the first Detroit Lions team in 1934.
COURTESY OF THE DETROIT LIONS

INTRODUCTION

SEVEN NFL TEAMS had head coaching vacancies after the 2020 season. There were recent Super Bowl winners (the Philadelphia Eagles), teams in major media markets (the New York Jets), teams with promising young quarterbacks (the Los Angeles Chargers), and teams about to get one with the No. 1 pick in the draft (the Jacksonville Jaguars).

But as Dan Campbell surveyed the landscape of available jobs, he told his agent there was one above all others he wanted—with the Detroit Lions.

Campbell spent parts of three seasons with the Lions during his 11-year playing career and identified with the city's blue-collar ethos. He knew how starved the fan base was for a winner, and what it would mean to give them one. And he appreciated the history of a franchise that has experienced more highs and lows than any other in the NFL.

"I think this is a special place," Campbell said at his introductory news conference on January 21, 2021. "I know when we bring a winner to this city, it's going to be something we can all be proud of."

The Lions are one of 13 NFL franchises to win four or more championships and one of three to go winless in a full season in the Super Bowl era. They've employed some of the greatest players to ever play the game, first-ballot Hall of Famers who would be legends in any era, and they suffered the worst tragedy imaginable on the field.

My goal in writing this book was to immerse you in all those moments, good and bad. The Lions are a storied franchise with a history that dates to the 1930s. They were an NFL power in the 1950s, they were one of the league's worst teams for decades, and they are chasing glory again under Campbell.

Lions Doak Walker (37), Bobby Layne (22), and head coach Buddy Parker, circa 1954.
COURTESY OF GETTY IMAGES

ACKNOWLEDGMENTS

I'VE COVERED the Detroit Lions for most of my adult life, since 2010 for the *Detroit Free Press* and at the *Oakland Press* for most of the 2007 and 2008 seasons before that. I've reported on much of what's in this book and leaned on the interactions I've had with past and current players to pare down 90 years of memorable games, important moments, and unique people in this franchise's indelible history.

Still, this work would not have been possible without the help of family, friends, and colleagues. The Lions have the best football communications staff in the business in Eamonn Reynolds, Solomon Williams, Greg Maiola, and Ellie Cross. They provided several photos for this book and aided my research on topics individually or through the comprehensive media guide they put out.

I spent countless hours at the Northville (Michigan) library doing research on many of the events I wasn't around to cover. The library has historical archives of the *Free Press* and other publications dating back to the 1800s. It was enlightening to see how the franchise evolved on the field and in its connection to the community through the lens of the news organizations that covered it. Support your local libraries and local news sources.

Pro Football Reference is the best place on the planet to check historical game and player facts. The Pro Football Hall of Fame and Professional Football Researchers Association have long been my compasses on the history of the organization and game. And my friend Jim Acho, a treasure trove of football history himself, facilitated a connection with Mel Farr Jr., who provided a photo of his dad and Lem Barney with the legendary Marvin Gaye.

I hope you enjoy this book and find it as comprehensive as I intend it to be.

Detail of the Lions' helmet worn by Jack Fox against the Minnesota Vikings at Ford Field on January 7, 2024.
COURTESY OF GETTY IMAGES

APRIL 3, 1934

HOW IT STARTED: FOOTBALL RETURNS TO DETROIT

DETROIT WAS no stranger to professional football when radio executive George A. Richards, the head of a syndicate of 23 local businessmen, wrote a check for $7,952.08 to buy the Portsmouth Spartans on April 3, 1934.

The Detroit Heralds, Detroit Panthers, and Detroit Wolverines all failed in the 1920s for financial or competitive reasons, but Richards and his group renamed the Spartans, a competitive NFL team from 1930 to 1933, the Lions—a jungle animal to pair with baseball's Detroit Tigers—and fielded an immediate winner.

The Lions, with former All-Pro quarterback Potsy Clark as coach and a roster made up mostly of ex-Spartans, won their first 10 games—seven by shutout—before losing three straight to close the year. They missed the playoffs after losing twice to the Chicago Bears in a four-day span, but played their home games at University of Detroit Stadium and thrilled crowds of more than 12,000 with their powerful single-wing offense.

"I can assure the fans of Detroit that we will have a high-class team. And by that I mean a winning team," Richards told the *Detroit Free Press* after his purchase in 1934. "I'm not predicting a title for Detroit, but we won't be far behind."

NOVEMBER 29, 1934

A THANKSGIVING TRADITION

AS THE OWNER of local radio station WJR, George A. Richards understood the value of promotion and programming. So with the Lions playing well on the field but still taking a back seat to the Tigers in the box office, he hatched a plan for his team to play its most important game of the season—against the defending world-champion Bears—on Thanksgiving Day, November 29, 1934.

With the 10–1 Lions facing an undefeated Bears team in a game that would decide the Western Division championship, Richards convinced the NBC Radio Network to carry the game coast-to-coast on its 94 stations.

The game sold out two weeks in advance. An estimated 26,000 fans filled University of Detroit Stadium for an 11 a.m. kickoff, many more were turned away at the gate, and the Bears rallied from a nine-point halftime deficit to beat the Lions, 19–16, on a trick pass from Bronco Nagurski to Bill Hewitt a few plays after a Lions interception.

The game was so good it started a tradition that continues to this day. The Lions have played 84 times on Thanksgiving entering the 2024 season, against 24 teams—most commonly the Green Bay Packers (22 games) and Bears (19)—and have a 37-45-2 record in a holiday game that's been played continuously since 1934 except during World War II.

The Dallas Cowboys started playing annually on Thanksgiving in 1966, and the NFL has since added a third Thanksgiving game. But the tradition got its start in Detroit and has never left despite occasional attempts by owners to take it away.

The Lions face the Bears in the first Thanksgiving Day game in 1934. The tradition continues to this day.
COURTESY OF THE DETROIT LIONS

1934

FEELING HONOLULU BLUE

GEORGE A. RICHARDS enlisted the help of one of his star players, tailback Glenn Presnell, to pick the Lions' new color scheme after the team moved to Detroit.

Presnell, who kicked a 54-yard field goal in 1934—an NFL record that stood for 19 years—told the *Associated Press* that Richards asked him and his wife, Liz, to choose from several jersey combinations he was considering for uniforms at the time he signed his contract. The couple picked a Honolulu shade of blue that Richards created to pair with silver pants, and the colors have been associated with the Lions nearly ever since.

The lone exception: When the Lions hired Alvin "Bo" McMillin as head coach from Indiana University in 1948, McMillin outfitted players in scarlet jerseys and white pants that resembled Indiana's color scheme, and added an all-black uniform that was only worn for important games. The change was short-lived, as the Lions went back to their Honolulu blue and silver uniforms for home games in 1949 and permanently in 1950.

Bill Dudley, left, with Coach Bo McMillan.
COURTESY OF GETTY IMAGES

DECEMBER 15, 1935

SWEET VICTORY: LIONS WIN FIRST TITLE

IT DIDN'T TAKE long for the Lions to win their first championship, but it didn't come easy.

The Packers went 8–4 and beat the Lions twice in 1935, but the Lions won the Western Division title with a 7–3–2 record because they had a higher winning percentage (ties were not factored into winning percentage at the time). All four teams in the division finished with winning records, and the Lions beat the Brooklyn Dodgers in their final game of the regular season to make the playoffs.

On December 15, 1935, the Lions hosted the New York Giants in the championship game on a rain- and sleet-filled day at University of Detroit Stadium. The Lions completed only two passes in the game but got rushing touchdowns from Dutch Clark, Ace Gutowsky, Ernie Caddel, and Buddy Parker to beat the Giants, 26–7.

Clark ran for 80 yards, while Parker, the future Lions coach, intercepted a pass to set up his touchdown. The Lions dominated the game in the trenches, and the unpleasant playing conditions helped slow the Giants' vaunted passing attack.

The 1935 Detroit Lions—the franchise's first championship team.
COURTESY OF THE DETROIT LIONS

1935

CITY OF CHAMPIONS: DETROIT REIGNS SUPREME

THE LIONS weren't the only Detroit sports team to win a championship in 1935. The city ruled the sports landscape of America.

At a time when Detroit and much of the nation were still in the throes of the Great Depression, the Lions won their first title in their second season of existence; the Tigers won the 1935 World Series; the Detroit Red Wings, still in their infancy as a franchise, won the Stanley Cup (in the 1935–36 season); and Detroit-raised Joe Louis was the undisputed best boxer in the world.

Detroit's dominance didn't stop with team sports. As the book *City of Champions* notes, Gar Wood, a legendary speedboat racer at the time, world champion checkers player Newell Banks, and even the Stroh's championship bowling team also hailed from the area, prompting the *Detroit Times* to dub Detroit "The City of Champions."

The moniker stuck. Then-Michigan Governor Frank D. Fitzgerald proclaimed a "Champions Day" to celebrate the city's sports successes on April 18, 1936. And Detroit has been known as one of the most rabid sports cities anywhere ever since.

The Lions went 7–3–2 in 1935 and beat the New York Giants in the championship game.
COURTESY OF THE DETROIT LIONS

1934–1938

DOUBLE DUTCH: LIONS' FIRST DO-IT-ALL STAR

THE LIONS' first star almost never played a down in Detroit.

Earl "Dutch" Clark retired from the Portsmouth Spartans before the 1933 season, with the team struggling financially, to become athletic director at the Colorado School of Mines. When the team moved to Detroit, the franchise acquired Clark's contract and the new ownership group made him one of the highest-paid players in the NFL to get him to return to football, though Clark continued coaching basketball for one season at the University of Colorado.

A two-time All-Pro with the Spartans, Clark played five seasons as a triple-threat back for the Lions and led the team to its first championship. He called plays on offense. He handled extra points and field goals and led the NFL in scoring three times. And he completed 53.5% of his passes in the 1936 season, at a time when the league average was 36.5%, according to the Pro Football Hall of Fame.

Though he had such poor eyesight he struggled to see his receivers downfield, Clark was one of three Lions named to the NFL's All-Decade team of the 1930s, along with Ox Emerson and George Christensen, and was a charter member of the Hall of Fame.

"Dutch" Clark in uniform for Colorado College.
COURTESY OF THE DETROIT LIONS

JANUARY 16, 1940

NEW MAN IN CHARGE

WITH GEORGE A. RICHARDS living in California and in failing health, the syndicate that brought the Lions to Detroit sold the team to Chicago department-store magnate Fred Mandel and two partners for $225,000 on January 16, 1940.

One of Mandel's first acts as owner was to bring back Potsy Clark as head coach. Clark resigned one season after leading the Lions to the 1935 championship, and he spent the next three years running the NFL's Dodgers with mixed results.

The 31-year-old Mandel, one of the NFL's first Jewish owners, promised to keep the Lions in Detroit, telling the *Free Press* on the day of the sale, "I regard Detroit as one of the country's foremost sports centers, and the team will stay here with local administration."

He sold the team eight years later to another conglomerate of local businessmen led by Edwin J. Anderson. Byron "Whizzer" White, the future Supreme Court justice, became the first Lion to lead the league in rushing in 1940, but the Lions posted just two winning records under Mandel's command.

Fred Mandel became part-owner of the Lions in 1940. He made good on his promise to keep the team in Detroit, but in his eight years as owner the team had six losing seasons.
COURTESY OF THE DETROIT LIONS

1944

FIREBALL FRANKIE: SINKWICH WINS MVP

AFTER AN 0–11 season in 1942, the first of two winless seasons in franchise history, the Lions took Georgia star and Heisman Trophy winner Frankie Sinkwich with the first pick of the 1943 draft.

On active duty with the U.S. Marines at the time, Sinkwich was discharged from the Marines due to flat feet and played two seasons with the Lions in 1943 and 1944 before joining the Army Air Force. Sinkwich was the Lions' first league MVP, winning the Joe F. Carr Award in 1944 when he finished third in the NFL in passing and rushing. His career was short-lived, however, as he injured his knee while playing for the Second Air Force Superbombers football team in 1945.

Sinkwich announced his retirement from football a few months later to run a café in his hometown of Youngstown, Ohio, and though he returned in 1946 to play four games for the New York Yankees football team, he never had the same impact again.

Frankie Sinkwich, then with the University of Georgia, signs a football for 12-year-old Clyde Wakelee as the Georgia team arrives at Pasadena for the annual Rose Bowl gridiron classic.
COURTESY OF GETTY IMAGES

1938–1946

CHIP OFF THE OL' BLOCK

BEFORE HE WAS a Hall of Fame center for the Lions, Alex Wojciechowicz was a member of Fordham University's famed "Seven Blocks of Granite," playing alongside future Hall of Fame coach Vince Lombardi on the school's legendary offensive line.

The sixth pick in the 1938 NFL draft, Wojciechowicz played both ways during his nine seasons in Detroit and rarely came off the field. He blocked for Frankie Sinkwich and Whizzer White on offense; he excelled as a linebacker on defense, where he intercepted a team-record seven passes in 1944; and he was known for his light-hearted humor in the locker room.

The Lions traded Wojciechowicz to the Philadelphia Eagles midway through the 1946 season, where he starred on defense and helped the Eagles win back-to-back championships in 1948–49. Once, Wojciechowicz played all 60 minutes of a game despite having two teeth knocked out.

In 1968, he joined Dutch Clark, Bill Dudley, and quarterback Bobby Layne as the fourth Lion enshrined in Canton.

The "Seven Blocks of Granite" that made up the line of Fordham's unbeaten 1937 team. Left to right: John "Tarzan" Druze, Al Babartsky, Vince Lombardi, Al Wojciechowicz, Nat Pierce, Ed Franco, and Leo Paquin.
COURTESY OF GETTY IMAGES

AUGUST 6, 1947

BULLET BILL: LIONS TRADE FOR HALL OF FAMER

BILL DUDLEY was at the top of his game when he announced his retirement after the 1946 season. Dudley was coming off an MVP year with the Pittsburgh Steelers, one in which he led the league in rushing, punt returns, and interceptions, but insisted his body wasn't built to take the pounding of playing football anymore.

The Lions sought permission to negotiate a contract with Dudley in July of 1947, and on August 6, after agreeing to a deal that would pay him $25,000 a year, acquired the do-it-all star in a massive trade involving five players and a future first-round draft pick.

Dudley scored 11 touchdowns in his first season with the Lions: two rushing, seven receiving, and one each on punt and interception returns. He spent two more years in Detroit before closing out his NFL career with two Pro Bowl seasons with Washington. In 1966 he was elected to the Hall of Fame, the second Lion to earn the honor.

Bill Dudley, circa 1940
COURTESY OF GETTY IMAGES

JANUARY 24, 1950

"NO PROFIT, NO LIONS"

TWO YEARS after Edwin J. Anderson and his group of prominent Michigan businessmen bought the Lions from Fred Mandel, he threatened to end his affiliation with the team amid sagging finances.

In a meeting of the team's 154 stockholders at the University Club on January 24, 1950, Anderson said the Lions lost $93,000 and $112,000 in successive years and called 1950 a "make or break" season for the team and ownership group.

"If Detroit fans do not support the type of team and the kind of football we will give them in 1950, then we are through," he said, according to the *Free Press*. "This is the last opportunity."

At the meeting, Anderson teased a big move coming that "figures to bring us another outstanding player with professional experience." Less than three months later, on April 8, 1950, the Lions acquired Bobby Layne, a star quarterback from the New York Yanks who would change the fortunes of the franchise for decades to come.

Football owners (from left), Edwin J. Anderson, Jack Mara, Victor Moarabito, and commissioner Pete Rozelle, circa 1960 at the Ambassador Hotel.
COURTESY OF GETTY IMAGES

89

Lions quarterback Bobby Layne making a pass against the Los Angeles Rams in Detroit.
COURTESY OF GETTY IMAGES

1950–1958

THE LEGEND OF BOBBY LAYNE

NEARLY 70 YEARS after he played his last game for the Lions, Bobby Layne is still considered the greatest quarterback in franchise history.

Layne was acquired in a 1950 trade for end Bob Mann; initially, the Lions sent fullback Camp Wilson to the Yanks in the deal, but Wilson refused to report and never played another down in the NFL. Layne played parts of nine seasons with the Lions, twice led the league in passing, and was part of four teams that reached NFL championship games and three that won titles.

Off the field, Layne was known for his hard-partying ways. In an interview on *The Tonight Show*, Colts defensive lineman Art Donovan once said that Layne's breath "reeked of whiskey" on the field. Donovan said he told Layne he must have had "a hell of a night" the night before, and that Layne replied he "had a few" at halftime.

On the field, Layne was known for his clutch play and competitiveness. He was runner-up for NFL MVP in 1956, was elected to the Hall of Fame 11 years later, and helped pioneer the two-minute offense.

"He demanded only the best and would accept only the best," Lions running back Doak Walker once said, according to the *Los Angeles Times*. "Here is a man who was a general on the field and off the field in every way. He was the greatest two-minute quarterback I have ever seen."

Layne finished his Lions career with 15,710 yards passing and played most of his final five NFL seasons with the Steelers.

1950s

THE MAKING OF A DYNASTY

THE LIONS were coming off four straight losing seasons when Edwin J. Anderson issued his threat at the team's shareholder meeting in 1950. Whether that was the spark or not, the franchise quickly became one of the NFL's two dominant teams of the decade.

The Lions went 6–6 in Bobby Layne's first season as quarterback in 1950, then had winning records in six of the next seven years and reached the NFL championship game in 1952–54 and 1957. The Cleveland Browns were the only team on par with the Lions in the '50s, claiming three titles and losing in four other championship games.

Ten players who played for the Lions in the decade have busts in the Hall of Fame, and Buddy Parker was a finalist for the Class of 2024, due largely to his 47–23–2 record as Lions coach. Parker's .671 winning percentage remains the second-best in franchise history, behind only Potsy Clark (.679).

Lions head coach Raymond "Buddy" Parker is lifted on the shoulders of linebacker Joe Schmidt and tackle Lou Creekmur after a 17–16 win over the Cleveland Browns in the 1953 championship game.
COURTESY OF GETTY IMAGES

DECEMBER 28, 1952

LIONS ARE CHAMPS AGAIN

THE LIONS ended a 17-year title drought when they beat the Browns, 17–7, on December 28, 1952, for their first of two straight championships. Bobby Layne scored the game's first touchdown on a 2-yard sneak in the second quarter, and the Lions defense came up with four big stops in the red zone.

The Browns, with an offense led by Hall of Famers Otto Graham and Marion Motley, outgained the Lions 384 yards to 258 but had one touchdown pass nullified because it was touched by two eligible receivers (which was illegal at the time), and Lou Groza missed three field goals.

Doak Walker, Layne's former teammate at Dallas's famed Highland Park High School, scored on a 67-yard run to give the Lions a 14–0 lead, and Pat Harder tacked on a 36-yard field goal after a Browns fumble.

More than 50,000 fans jammed Cleveland's Municipal Stadium for the game, and the Lions were greeted at Michigan Central station after their train ride home that night by what the *Free Press* called a "joyous mob" of more than 400 fans waving pennants and carrying portable radios.

Jubilant Lions rejoice in their dressing room after their 17–7 win over the Cleveland Browns.
COURTESY OF GETTY IMAGES

DECEMBER 27, 1953

BOBBY GOES BACK-TO-BACK

THE LIONS and Browns faced off again for the NFL championship on December 27, 1953, this time at Detroit's Briggs Stadium, in a game that helped cement Bobby Layne's status as one of the most clutch late-game quarterbacks in NFL history.

The Lions got another stellar effort from their defense, holding Otto Graham to 2 of 15 passing for a net of 4 yards, but still trailed by six points late in the fourth quarter after Layne had a touchdown catch nullified by penalty on an impromptu halfback pass from Doak Walker.

Layne, playing through an arm injury, led a late touchdown drive, finding Jim Doran for the tying score on a 33-yard pass with about 2 minutes to play on a possession the *Free Press* said was marred "by flying fists that embroiled virtually every member of both squads." Doran, who caught just six passes with no touchdowns in the regular season, had three catches for 68 yards on the go-ahead drive.

Walker kicked the extra point to give the Lions a 17–16 lead, and Carl Karilivacz had a game-clinching interception on the ensuing possession as the Lions became the sixth repeat champion in NFL history.

Bobby Layne looks to pass in a 17–16 win over the Cleveland Browns in the 1953 NFL championship game at Briggs Stadium in Detroit.

COURTESY OF GETTY IMAGES

Cleveland Browns' fullback Jim Brown tries to hurdle the Detroit line but is stopped by Lions linebacker Joe Schmidt.
COURTESY OF GETTY IMAGES

1953–1965

NO ORDINARY JOE

THE LIONS of the 1950s were known for their dominant defenses, and no one epitomized those units more than Joe Schmidt.

A seventh-round pick out of the University of Pittsburgh in 1953, Schmidt was a nine-time team captain and eight-time first-team All-Pro who made 10 straight Pro Bowls from 1954 to 1963. He had 24 career interceptions, recovered 17 fumbles, and saved some of his biggest plays for the playoffs.

As a rookie, Schmidt forced an Otto Graham fumble to set up the Lions' first touchdown in their 1953 title game win over the Browns. He had an interception in the 1954 championship game, and another three years later in 1957.

Schmidt played 13 seasons for the Lions and spent another six years as the team's head coach. He was named to the NFL's all-decade team of the 1950s and was voted one of its top 100 players of all time. He started his career as an outside linebacker but moved inside in 1955 where his rangy play and sure tackling helped define the middle linebacker position in the early days of the 4-3 defense.

Beyond his contributions on the field, Schmidt made a significant impact off of it. He helped organize what's now known as the NFL Players Association in the 1950s and was a leading force in getting players training-camp pay and pensions.

"He was the best," said Gene Cronin, Schmidt's teammate with the Lions from 1956 to 1959. "Years ago, there was a story going around that they were going to make a movie called *The Violent World of Sam Huff*. And (Huff) was a fine middle linebacker, no question about it. And they asked Gino Marchetti, they said, 'What do you think about them making a movie called *The Violent World of Sam Huff*?' And he said, 'Well, if they make a movie, they better get Joe Schmidt to play the part.'"

1951–1958

CHRIS'S CREW, AND A RETURN MAN, TOO

JOE SCHMIDT was the leader of the Lions defense, but he was far from the unit's only star.

Jack Christiansen was a six-time first-team All-Pro selection who twice led the NFL in interceptions. He picked off 12 passes for the 1953 Lions, had 46 interceptions in his career, and was a spectacular punt returner who scored eight touchdowns before teams stopped kicking his way.

As a rookie in 1951, Christiansen returned two punts for touchdowns of 47 and 69 yards in a game against the Los Angeles Rams. Later in the season, he returned two more punts for scores (of 71 and 89 yards) in a game against the Packers.

Christiansen initially went to college to run track and only got talked into playing football in his sophomore year at Colorado State. But he became the leader of a Lions' secondary that was nicknamed "Chris's Crew" and was elected to the Hall of Fame in the Class of 1970.

Safety Jack Christiansen intercepts quarterback Otto Graham's pass to Dante Lavelli in a 56–10 loss to the Cleveland Browns during the league championship game on December 26, 1954.
COURTESY OF GETTY IMAGES

DECEMBER 26, 1954

THE ONE THAT GOT AWAY

THE LIONS and Browns were the most dominant teams of the 1950s, but their rivalry was largely one-sided. The Lions won seven of the eight meetings between the teams in the decade, with the lone exception coming in the 1954 title game.

On December 26, 1954, with Otto Graham playing what was supposed to be the last game of his Hall of Fame career, the Browns spoiled the Lions' bid for a three-peat with a 56–10 thrashing at Cleveland's Municipal Stadium. Bobby Layne threw six interceptions, three that deflected off Lions players, and Graham accounted for six touchdowns (three rushing) in a game that came one week after the Lions beat the Browns 14–10 to close the regular season.

Graham finished 9 of 12 passing for 163 yards and left late in the game to a standing ovation. The Lions' Charley Ane and the Browns' Carlton Massey were ejected when tempers flared in the fourth quarter "and the game became a boxing match," according to the *Free Press*. And the defeat went down as the most lopsided of Parker's coaching career.

"They just beat the hell out of us," Layne told the *Free Press* after the game, sitting in front of his locker with his shoulders slumped and a cigarette in his mouth.

In the 1954 NFL championship, Cleveland Browns quarterback Otto Graham attempts a pass against the Lions in Cleveland on December 26.
COURTESY OF GETTY IMAGES

1954

DUTY CALLS FOR LARY

THE LIONS lost four players to military service commitments before the 1954 season: Oliver Spencer and Pence Dacus to the Air Force and Gene Gedman and Yale Lary to the Army.

Lary left the team for Fort Benning, Georgia, in May of 1954, and his absence left two gaping holes in the Lions' roster for the next two seasons. Enshrined in the Hall of Fame in the Class of 1979, Lary was one of the NFL's best punters and a staple of the Lions defense playing alongside Jack Christiansen at right safety during the first half of his career.

A third-round pick out of Texas A&M in 1952, Lary won three NFL punting titles and averaged 44.3 yards per punt for his career, second only to Sammy Baugh at the time of his retirement. He's one of 39 players in NFL history with at least 50 interceptions. And he scored three career touchdowns on punt returns.

The Lions sagged to a 3–9 record in 1955 but were back among the best teams in football when Lary returned in 1956. Lary spent that summer playing pro baseball in the Texas League, and he had eight interceptions—tied with Christiansen and Washington's Norb Hecker for second-most in the league—in his first season back on the field.

The Lions' Yale Lary punts during the 1957 NFC championship game.
COURTESY OF GETTY IMAGES

A DAY FOR DOAK

IT TOOK TWO trades for the Lions to land one of the best running backs in franchise history, but no one dared complain after Doak Walker helped the franchise win two championships.

Walker, the 1948 Heisman Trophy winner at SMU, was a first-round pick by the Boston Yanks in the 1949 NFL draft and a ninth-round choice by the Browns in the AAFC draft the same year. The Lions acquired Walker from the Yanks for fullback Johnny Rauch, but when the Browns changed leagues in 1950, NFL commissioner Bert Bell urged the Lions to work out a deal with Cleveland, too, according to the Professional Football Researchers Association.

The Lions sent a second-round pick to the Browns in 1950 for Walker's exclusive rights, and Walker quickly became one of the best all-purpose players in the league. He made the Pro Bowl five times, was a four-time first-team All-Pro selection, and led the league in scoring twice in his six NFL seasons. Walker also shined in two Lions championship-game wins over the Browns, scoring the winning touchdown in the 1952 title game and accounting for 11 of the Lions' 17 points in 1953.

Walker retired in 1955 to devote his time to his extensive business interests in Dallas. The Lions designated their last game of that season "Doak Walker Day" and retired his No. 37 jersey in a halftime ceremony at Briggs Stadium.

Doak Walker carries the ball for the Lions in a 1951 game against the San Francisco 49ers.
COURTESY OF GETTY IMAGES

1957–1959

A HALL OF A TRADE

DOAK WALKER wasn't the only Hall of Fame running back the Lions acquired via trade. On May 14, 1957, the team sent second-year fullback Bill Bowman and defensive halfback Bill Stits to the San Francisco 49ers for John Henry Johnson and a 1958 draft pick.

A powerful runner and capable receiver who was part of the 49ers' famed Million Dollar Backfield, Johnson immediately took over as Lions' starting fullback and led the team with 621 yards rushing in his first season in Detroit. He played the 1957–59 seasons with the Lions before he was traded to the Steelers, where he had his greatest success as a pro.

Johnson made three Pro Bowls and had two 1,000-yard rushing seasons in Pittsburgh and was elected to the Hall of Fame in 1987.

The Lions made one other important trade before the start of the 1957 season, sending three offensive linemen and halfback Don McIlhenny to the Packers for quarterback Tobin Rote. Rote led the NFL in passing in 1956 but was deemed expendable in Green Bay due to the presence of Bart Starr.

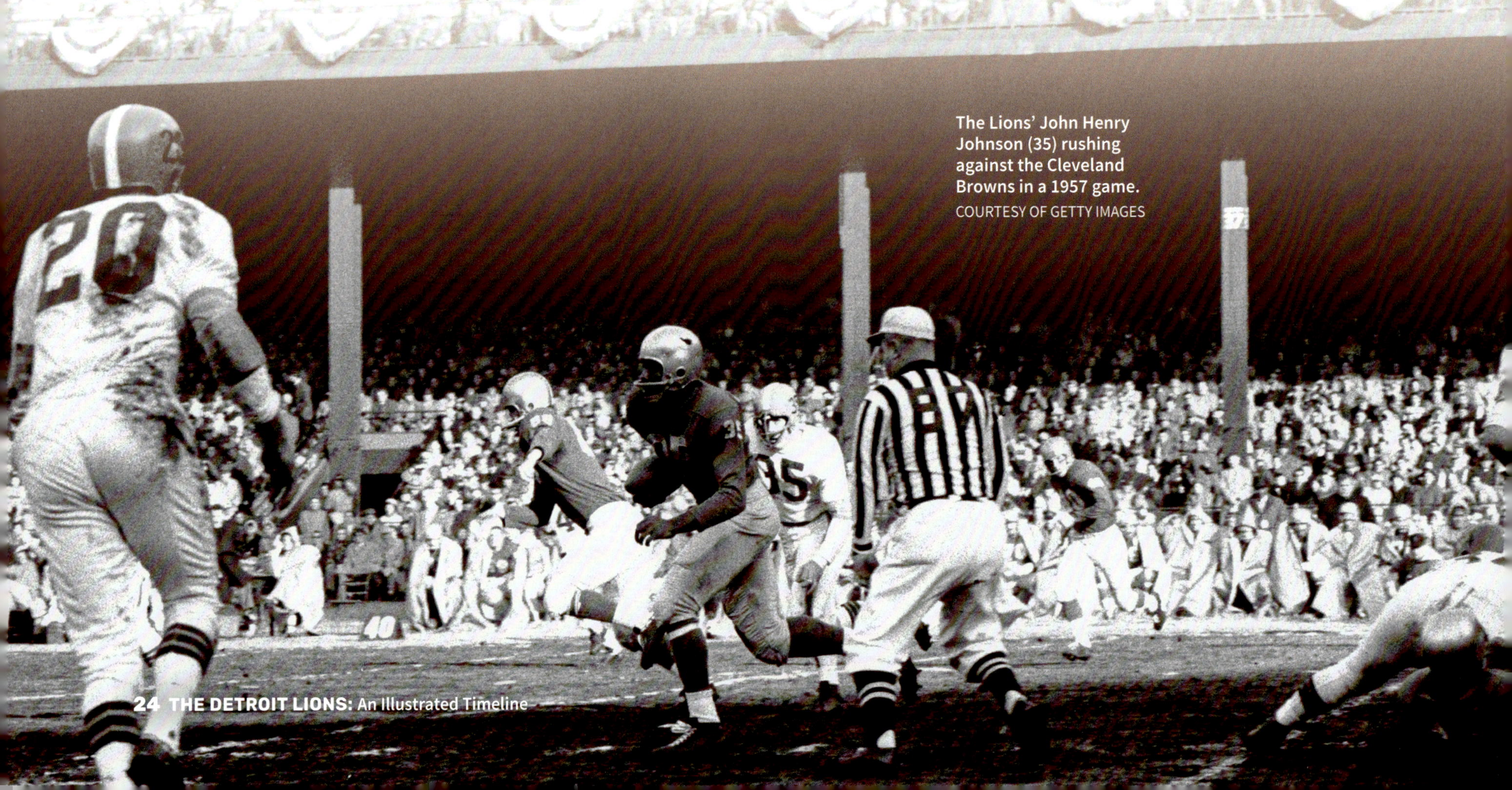

The Lions' John Henry Johnson (35) rushing against the Cleveland Browns in a 1957 game.
COURTESY OF GETTY IMAGES

AUGUST 12, 1957

BUDDY SAYS BYE-BYE

BUDDY PARKER joined the Lions in 1951 and won two championships in his six seasons in Detroit before leaving abruptly less than 48 hours before the 1957 exhibition opener.

At the team's annual Meet the Lions banquet that summer at the Detroit Statler Hotel, Parker stunned his players and others in the organization when he told a crowd of about 600 fans he was quitting the team.

Parker's resignation was reportedly due to several factors: He was frustrated with some players and their hard-partying ways, his influence in the organization was waning, and he was feuding with one faction of the team's board of directors. The tipping point, said ex-Lions defensive lineman Roger Zatkoff, who was at the banquet that night awaiting his trade to Detroit, came when Parker happened upon players fraternizing with board members and fans at the hotel against his wishes.

"All of a sudden he said (he quit) and walked off and, what do you do?" Lions receiver Jerry Reichow said. "No one had ever been through that before. We didn't know what to say or what to do, so then we went out and got beat the first game. It was quite a year."

George Wilson, Parker's long-time assistant, took over as head coach and stayed in that spot for eight years.

George Wilson (left) and Buddy Parker at the Pro Bowl coaches luncheon on January 9, 1958.
COURTESY OF GETTY IMAGES

DECEMBER 8, 1957

BREAK A LEG

THE LIONS were fortunate to have two good quarterbacks on their roster in 1957, Bobby Layne and Tobin Rote, and they needed both to reach their fourth championship game in six seasons.

Layne was under center in the second quarter of a December 8 game against the Browns that year when he was hit by three defenders as he rolled out to pass and fractured the fibula in his right leg.

In the hospital after the game, Layne shooed away doctors so he could watch the rival 49ers on TV.

"He's got his football pants on, a Marlboro cigarette in his mouth, he had an ice pack on his ankle, and he's watching the 49ers game," Gene Cronin recalled in a 2017 interview. "He was rattling on, the doctor comes over, he said, 'Mr. Layne, we need . . .' (And Bobby said,) 'You get out of here. . . . I told you not to bother me until this game's over.' And he ran the damn doctor out of the room. . . . Toughest old guy I ever saw."

Rote, who made five starts in 1957 and had more touchdown passes than Layne (11 to six), threw a third-quarter touchdown pass to Dave Middleton to lead the Lions to a 20–7 victory and quarterbacked the team in the playoffs.

Lions quarterback Tobin Rote (18) making a pass against the Cleveland Browns in the NFL championship in Detroit.
COURTESY OF GETTY IMAGES

DECEMBER 22, 1957

THE COMEBACK KIDS

THE 1957 SEASON was no cakewalk for the Lions. They went 8–4 in the regular season and rallied from double-digit deficits to win two of those games. Their greatest adversity, however, came three days before Christmas in the Western Division championship game against the 49ers at San Francisco's Kezar Stadium.

Y. A. Tittle threw three touchdown passes in the first half of that game to stake the 49ers to a 24–7 halftime lead. The 49ers were so confident they were headed to the championship game that they began celebrating in the locker room.

"It was only a two-by-four wall with drywall on either side with vents that were between the two [locker rooms]," Roger Zatkoff recalled in 2017. "You could hear the guy buying his wife a fur coat, another one buying a car, another one had to get his championship tickets. The game was over as far as they were concerned."

Fueled by the celebration they heard through the walls, the Lions held the 49ers to a field goal on the opening drive of the second half and then scored 24 unanswered points for a 31–27 victory. A week later, they would face the Browns for the fourth and final time in a championship game.

The 49ers' Billy Wilson snags a pass from QB Y. A. Tittle that was good for a touchdown in the second quarter of a clash with the Lions at Kezar Stadium for the NFL Western Division title.
COURTESY OF GETTY IMAGES

DECEMBER 29, 1957

A CHAMPIONSHIP BLOWOUT

AFTER THE Lions beat the 49ers, more than 3,000 fans camped overnight outside Briggs Stadium in 20-degree temperatures to get tickets to the championship game, which was blacked out on local TV.

The Lions didn't disappoint those who showed up to the December 29 game, avenging their 1954 loss with a 59–14 win over the Browns that remains one of the most lopsided title games in NFL history.

The Lions intercepted five passes, recovered two fumbles, and held Jim Brown, the NFL's MVP that season as a rookie, to 69 yards rushing on 20 carries. Terry Barr returned an interception 19 yards for a touchdown. Steve Junker scored on a fake field goal. And Tobin Rote ran for one touchdown and had 280 yards passing and four more scores as Bobby Layne watched from the sideline on crutches with a cast on his leg.

After the game, Joe Schmidt was hoisted on the shoulders of fans who rushed the field to celebrate what remains the Lions' last championship.

"It was one of those games where we couldn't do anything wrong and the Browns couldn't do anything right," Jerry Reichow said in 2017. "It was a funny deal, strange deal. Strange year, actually."

Joe Schmidt is carried off the field by fans after the Lions beat the Browns in the 1957 championship game.
COURTESY OF GETTY IMAGES

OCTOBER 6, 1958

THE CURSE OF BOBBY LAYNE

THINGS GOT stranger on October 6, 1958, two games into the defense of their title, when the Lions traded Bobby Layne to the Steelers for quarterback Earl Morrall and two draft picks in a move so stunning it made over-the-masthead news in one local paper.

Joe Schmidt told the *Free Press* the deal "makes me sick. I think it's a big mistake. He's still a damned good quarterback." Pro Bowl offensive lineman Lou Creekmur called it "a big shock" and "a debatable trade." And Layne himself expressed disappointment at the deal.

"It hurts me . . . it hurts quite a bit," he told the *Free Press* after the trade. "I haven't much complaint I guess . . . but regardless of what people think of me, I gave my heart and soul to football."

Years later, Schmidt recalled Layne being "pretty bitter" about the trade, which marked the end of the franchise's dynasty—and if you believe in legend, doomed the Lions to decades of disappointment.

Layne supposedly cursed the franchise to 50 years of bad luck on his way out the door, saying the Lions would never win a championship without him, though there is little record of the curse other than a 1971 television interview unearthed by *Peyton's Places*.

"Well, it hurt me naturally when I was traded to the Steelers from the Lions," Layne said in the clip. "We'd been very successful with Detroit. I really didn't know what to think. I tried what they refer to as a hex."

The trade of Bobby Layne to the Steelers brought the Lions Earl Morrall . . . and a curse that lasted over 50 years.
COURTESY OF THE DETROIT LIONS

According to reports at the time, the Lions traded Layne amid an 0–1–1 start after George Wilson appeared at a fan club luncheon where he criticized Layne's judgement on an option play in the final two minutes of the previous day's game against the Packers. The *Detroit News* reported the hard-partying Layne also showed up drunk to a team meeting.

Whatever the case, Layne's teammates said years later they believed in the curse, and the Lions won only one playoff game in the first 65 years after the trade.

The Lions' Lou Creekmur in the locker room after a game against the Cleveland Browns in Detroit.
COURTESY OF GETTY IMAGES

THE IRONMAN RETIRES

WHEN LOU CREEKMUR announced his plans to retire midway through his ninth NFL season in 1958, he had never missed a game or practice—and it wasn't because he never got hurt. A six-time first-team All-Pro, Creekmur played one season with a crushed sternum and had 16 or 17 concussions in his career, he told the Concussion Legacy Foundation.

The ironman of the Lions' 1950s run of dominance, Creekmur started as an offensive guard before moving to left tackle and also doubled as a short-yardage and goal-line defender most of his career. In 1953, he was selected first-team All-Pro at both guard and tackle. And in 1955, when he earned second-team All-Pro honors, he spent most of the season as a defensive middle guard due to injuries.

The Lions had two Hall of Fame linemen on their offensive front in the early part of the decade, Creekmur and Dick Stanfel. In 1956, they sent Stanfel, MVP of the team's 1953 championship season, to Washington as part of a four-team trade that brought back defensive lineman Ray Krouse from the Giants so they could move Creekmur back to left tackle.

Creekmur retired after the 1958 season with 108 consecutive games played. After starting 0–4 in 1959, the Lions talked Creekmur into returning for the final eight games before he retired for good at the end of the season.

1950s–2010s

ONE-AND-DONES IN CANTON

OF THE 23 Hall of Fame players to suit up for the Lions, four played only a single season with the team.

Frank Gatski started at center on the Lions' 1957 championship team and was part of a line that also featured Lou Creekmur at left tackle, but Gatski was best known as a three-time first-team All-Pro selection with the Browns. Fullback Ollie Matson, who won two Olympic medals in track in 1952, played one season near the end of his career for the Lions (in 1963) and had minimal impact (13 carries, 20 yards).

Star 49ers halfback Hugh McElhenny followed Matson to Detroit in 1964 for the final season of his career. And pass rusher Dwight Freeney played the final five games of his career for the Lions in 2017.

Curly Culp, a nose tackle who helped the Kansas City Chiefs win Super Bowl IV, appeared in five games with the Lions in 1962 and 1963. The Lions claimed Culp after he was cut by the Houston Texans late in the 1980 season, and Culp appeared in two games as a backup in 1981.

Ollie Matson spent the prime years of his Hall of Fame career in Chicago, but played for the Lions in 1963.
COURTESY OF GETTY IMAGES

1962

SECOND BEST IN '62

AS GOOD as the Lions of the 1950s were, Joe Schmidt said in 2017 one of the best teams he played on was the 1962 Lions team that didn't make the playoffs.

The Lions went 11–3 that season but finished second in the West behind the 13–1 Packers. The Packers beat the Giants in the championship game to win their second title in as many seasons, but their dynasty of the 1960s might be remembered differently if not for an errant pass in their 9–7 win over the Lions that October.

In a battle of 3–0 teams on a rainy day at Green Bay's City Stadium, the Lions led 7–6 late in the game when George Wilson called a pass play on third-and-7 from around midfield. Terry Barr ran a 12-yard route but slipped on the wet field as Milt Plum threw the ball in his direction. Herb Adderly intercepted the pass and returned it to the Lions' 18-yard line. After two runs, Paul Hornung kicked the game-winning field goal, his third of the game.

The Lions beat the Packers on Thanksgiving that season to account for Green Bay's only loss, and though they lost the season finale to the Bears, 3–0, they would have won the conference and gone on to the title game had they beaten the Packers in Week 4.

"I always look back on that '62 team, I just felt that we had as good a team as Green Bay or even better," Schmidt said.

Paul Hornung (5) of the Green Bay Packers carries the ball against Carl Brettschneider (57), Joe Schmidt (56), Yale Lary (28), Roger Brown (76), and Wayne Walker (55) of the Lions during a 1962 game in Green Bay.
COURTESY OF GETTY IMAGES

1960s

THE ORIGINAL FEARSOME FOURSOME

THE LIONS finished second behind the Packers in the Western Conference in three straight seasons from 1960 to 1962. They never ranked higher than seventh in the 14-team league in scoring, but they always had one of the best defenses in football.

With Joe Schmidt nearing the end of his Hall of Fame career and new faces dotting the secondary, the strength of the Lions defense was a line radio announcer Van Patrick nicknamed the "Fearsome Foursome."

Sacks did not become an official stat until 1982, but the unit of Alex Karras, Roger Brown, Darris McCord, and Bill Glass combined for 38 sacks in 1961, according to Pro Football Reference. In their Thanksgiving win over the Packers that season they had what news reports at the time described as 10 or 11 sacks on Starr.

Karras, who was elected posthumously to the Hall of Fame in 2020, and Brown, a six-time Pro Bowler with the Lions and Rams, were considered two of the best defensive tackles in football. Sam Williams, a backup in 1960 and 1961, replaced Glass in the Fearsome Foursome in 1962, and the group stayed intact until 1966 when the Atlanta Falcons took Williams and two other Lions in the expansion draft.

The Packers' Bart Starr (15) tries to elude Lions defenders Darris McCord (78), Alex Karras (71), and Roger Brown (76) during the second quarter of a game in 1962. Detroit won the game, 26–14.
COURTESY OF GETTY IMAGES

Defensive tackle Alex Karras during the Lions' 31–7 victory over the Los Angeles Rams on October 31, 1965 in Los Angeles.
COURTESY OF GETTY IMAGES

1963

KARRAS SUSPENDED FOR A SEASON

A MEMBER of the NFL's all-decade team of the 1960s, Alex Karras likely would have been inducted to the Pro Football Hall of Fame sooner had he and Paul Hornung not been suspended for the 1963 season for gambling.

Karras admitted in a national television interview in January of that year he bet on games, and while he insisted it was only for cigars and cigarettes, the admission prompted an investigation that lasted more than three months, involved at least 52 interviews, and resulted in some players taking lie-detector tests to prove they did not unduly influence games.

Then–NFL commissioner Pete Rozelle found that Karras, the loveable but headstrong character who went on to an acting career and played the role of Mongo in *Blazing Saddles*, bet $50 or $100 on games on at least six occasions, and five other Lions—Joe Schmidt, Sam Williams, John Gordy, Wayne Walker, and Gary Lowe—wagered $50 on the 1962 championship game while watching it with Karras at the Florida home of a friend who was involved with dog racing.

Rozelle said the group was guilty of "bad judgment"—Karras also owned a stake in a local Detroit bar frequented by known gamblers—but that no one bet against his team, sold information to gamblers, or fixed games. He fined the five players $2,000 each and the Lions organization twice that. Karras was reinstated after one year and went on to play seven more seasons for the Lions, earning first- or second-team All-Pro honors in five of those years.

NOVEMBER 22, 1963

WILLIAM CLAY FORD TAKES OVER ON A TRAGIC DAY

THE LIONS have been owned by the Ford family for more than six decades, since William Clay Ford, the grandson of auto pioneer Henry Ford, made a surprise bid of $6 million for sole control of the team at a board of directors meeting in October 1963.

Ford was team president at the time, and one of the organization's 144 shareholders. The idea to buy the team outright came from his brother, Henry, who watched an incensed Ford put his foot through his TV while watching a 1961 game at his mansion.

The board approved the sale less than two weeks after Ford's bid, and shareholders voted to accept the offer in a meeting at the Statler Hilton Hotel on November 22, 1963—the same day president John F. Kennedy was assassinated.

"It's a terrible coincidence that both of these things would occur around the same time," Ford told the *Free Press* in 2003. "There were a couple of times over the years when some things happened to us that you just couldn't figure out why or how it happened, and you'd briefly think if there's some kind of stigma attached to anything else that may have taken place that awful day."

Ford's legacy as Lions owner is a complicated one. He was a lifelong Lions fan who was friendly and generous with players and team employees, but the Lions won only one playoff game during his tenure and he was frustratingly loyal to a string of poor coaches and general managers.

William Clay Ford owned the Lions from 1963 until 2014.
COURTESY OF THE DETROIT LIONS

Ford owned the team until his death March 9, 2014, though his son, Bill Jr., had a prominent role running the team in his later years. Ford's wife, Martha Firestone Ford, took over as controlling owner after Ford's passing, and after a multiyear apprenticeship Ford's daughter, Sheila Ford Hamp, took over as principal owner and chair on June 23, 2020.

1960–1965

NIGHT TRAIN AND THE NECKTIE

DICK "NIGHT TRAIN" LANE was considered one of the best cornerbacks in the NFL when he came to the Lions in 1960. He led the league with a still-record 14 interceptions as a rookie with the Rams in 1952, and he led it again two years later when he had 10 picks for the Chicago Cardinals.

A risk-taker in coverage who made three Pro Bowls in six seasons with the Lions, Lane's signature clothesline tackle was known as the Night Train Necktie, and his style of play forced the league to enact rule changes that made the game safer.

In 1962, the NFL disallowed tackling by the facemask after Lane made a particularly gruesome play on Rams receiver Jon Arnett. Lane took a flying leap at Arnett and yanked him to the ground by the facemask. Arnett lay unmoving for several "scary" minutes after the hit, according to news reports, until he was awakened by smelling salts.

Lane, who earned his nickname because of a song by the same name he played repeatedly in training camp as a rookie, was second on the career interceptions list (68) behind Emlen Tunnell when he retired after the 1965 season. He was a part-time player his final two years in the NFL, spending time on the Lions' taxi squad after suffering a knee injury in 1964. He was enshrined in the Hall of Fame in 1974.

Night Train Lane's clothesline tackle of the Rams' Jon Arnett in 1961 led to a rule change the following year.
COURTESY OF GETTY IMAGES

AUGUST 3, 1963

THE PAPER LION CRUMBLES

A YEAR after they came within a whisker of winning the West, the Lions gave rise to one of the most famous sports books of all time: *Paper Lion: Confessions of a Last-String Quarterback* by George Plimpton.

A Harvard-educated author and socialite, Plimpton spent part of the 1963 training camp with the Lions as a backup quarterback and then chronicled his time with the team in two essays for *Sports Illustrated* and the book he published in 1966, which was later turned into a movie. He wore No. 0 and wrote that when Sam Williams approached him before the first preseason game and said, "That's a good number you're wearing," he replied, "It indicates my talent."

Plimpton got a unique look at the Lions' training and social habits and even appeared in an intra-squad scrimmage at Pontiac's Wisner Stadium on August 3, 1963. He played five plays, fumbled once, was sacked twice, threw one incomplete pass, and the offense lost yardage the fifth time on a running play. Plimpton dressed for a preseason game a week later, but after Pete Rozelle sent word he couldn't play in the game, he cleaned out his locker and left the team.

George Plimpton on the bench during Lions training camp.
COURTESY OF GETTY IMAGES

JANUARY 11, 1967

SCHMIDT TAKES OVER AS COACH

HARRY GILMER, a backup quarterback with the Lions in 1955 and 1956, spent two seasons as head coach of the team a decade later and posted back-to-back losing records before William Clay Ford turned to Joe Schmidt, the legendary linebacker, as his replacement.

Initially brought on board to fill the newly created position of linebackers coach after his retirement in 1966, Schmidt spent one season apprenticing for the head job before taking over in 1967. He inherited a Lions team beset by player squabbles and discipline issues, and after two lean years he had the team back competing for the division title.

Schmidt surrounded himself with veteran assistants like Chuck Knox and Jim David. He told the team website in 2023 he never had any ambition to coach, but he compiled a 43-35-7 record (.558) with one playoff appearance over six seasons. He quit in 1973 after butting heads over the roster with Russ Thomas, the longtime Lions executive who famed *Free Press* columnist Mitch Albom once described as being a "general manager with the skills of an accountant."

No Lions coach who has coached at least one full season has a higher winning percentage since.

Hall of Fame enshrinee Joe Schmidt (right) poses with his bronze bust and presenter William Clay Ford during the Pro Hall of Fame enshrinement ceremony on July 28, 1973 in Canton, Ohio.
COURTESY OF THE DETROIT LIONS

SEPTEMBER 17, 1967

"THIS IS GOING TO BE EASY"

THE LIONS hit the jackpot with their first three picks of the 1967 draft, taking Mel Farr, a running back out of UCLA, in Round 1; Lem Barney, a cornerback from Jackson State, in Round 2; and Paul Naumoff, a linebacker from Tennessee, in Round 3. By 1970 all three had made at least one Pro Bowl, and Barney had established himself as one of the best defensive backs in football.

Barney had one of the most memorable Lions debuts ever, intercepting a Bart Starr pass that he returned 24 yards for a touchdown on the first pass thrown his way in the first quarter of his first NFL game.

"I dove in front of him, got up and ran in the end zone for (24) yards for a touchdown," Barney told the team website years later. "I looked up to the sky as I slammed the ball down and I said, 'Lord, this is going to be easy.'"

Everything seemed to come easy for Barney, who returned kicks and punts and served as the Lions' punter as a rookie. He tied for the league lead with 10 interceptions that year, returning three for touchdowns, and was named the first ever Associated Press NFL Defensive Rookie of the Year.

Barney, the first of three legendary No. 20s in Detroit, finished his 11-year career with 56 interceptions. Fifteen years after retiring, he was enshrined in the Hall of Fame.

Lem Barney looks on from the sidelines during an NFL football game circa 1968. Barney played for the Lions from 1967–77.
COURTESY OF GETTY IMAGES

BROTHERLY LOVE: SIBLINGS AND TEAMMATES AS LIONS

MEL FARR won NFL Offensive Rookie of the Year in 1967, when he led the Lions in rushing yards (860) and receptions (39) and made the Pro Bowl the first of two times in his career.

He was on pace for an even better season in 1968 when he suffered the first of two knee injuries that cut short his career. He played only seven games in 1968 and five in 1969, but stayed in Detroit long enough to play with his brother, Miller, for one season in 1973.

The Farrs are one of six sets of brothers known to have played for the Lions in the same season. The others are Jim and Ralph Jones in 1946, Alex and Ted Karras in 1965, Darnell and Marquis Walker in 2000, Romeo and Julian Okwara in 2020–23, and Shane and Brandon Zylstra in 2022.

Mel's son Mike also played for the Lions, catching 69 passes in 30 starts from 1990 to 1992.

Lions linebackers Julian Okwara (99) and Romeo Okwara (95) celebrate a play during a 2023 preseason football game against the Giants.
COURTESY OF GETTY IMAGES

1971

MUSIC TO MARVIN'S EARS

ROOKIE-OF-THE-YEAR AWARDS weren't the only honors Lem Barney and Mel Farr won during their time with the Lions. The duo also received gold records for their performance on the Motown hit "What's Going On" by Marvin Gaye.

A self-acknowledged "frustrated athlete," Gaye played one-on-one basketball with Jim Brown, scrimmaged for a week with the Eastern Michigan football team, and pleaded for a tryout with the Lions only to have the team say no.

Gaye was close friends with some of Detroit's most high-profile athletes, including Barney, Farr, and Detroit Pistons legend Dave Bing. In 1971 he told the *Free Press* he was sitting around drinking beer, arguing about who could sing and who couldn't when he impulsively asked Barney and Farr to help on an album that went on to sell more than 2 million copies.

"Lem can sing. . . . He's sort of legitimate," Gaye told the *Free Press*. "I don't know if Mel had any experience, but he snaps his fingers real well."

COURTESY OF GETTY IMAGES

COURTESY OF MEL FARR JR.

Marvin Gaye had two Lions players sing backup on his 1971 hit "What's Going On?"

NOVEMBER 8, 1970

TOM DEMPSEY'S RECORD-SETTING KICK

WHEN THE New Orleans Saints sent Tom Dempsey out for a 63-yard field goal with 2 seconds left in a November 1970 game at Tulane Stadium, Joe Schmidt thought the try was so preposterously long he was expecting a trick play.

Bert Rechicahar held the NFL record at the time with a 56-yard field goal set in 1953, and the Lions had blocked a kick by Dempsey, who was born without toes on his right foot, earlier in the game.

Dempsey lined up at his own 34-yard line, shuffled his feet and took two steps forward at the snap, and boomed the ball just over the goalpost at the front of the Lions end zone to give the Saints an improbable 19–17 win.

Dempsey said after the game he knew he could kick the ball that far, but maybe not that straight, and a stunned Wayne Walker called the kick "a miracle."

"Bobby Thompson's home run, nothing compares to it," Walker told the *Free Press* after the game.

Dempsey's heroics might not have been necessary if not for an officiating error one series earlier, when the Lions took a 17–16 lead on Errol Mann's 17-yard field goal with 11 seconds to play. Officials lost track of downs on that possession, and Greg Landry completed a drive-extending third-down pass on what would have otherwise been a long field goal try on fourth down.

The Saints' Tom Dempsey watches one of his kicks split the uprights during the first half against the Lions. Dempsey kicked four field goals—the final kick with 2 seconds left, a record 63 yards to give the Saints a come-from-behind victory 19–17.
COURTESY OF GETTY IMAGES

DECEMBER 20, 1970

BARNEY'S BIG DAY HELPS SECURE WILD CARD

WHEN THE NFL and AFL merged in 1970, the 26-team league reformatted as two 13-team conferences with three divisions each and the playoffs expanded to include the three division winners in each conference plus one wild card.

The Lions finished 10–4 that season, two games behind the Vikings in the NFC Central but with the best record of the NFC's non-division winners. They secured the NFC's first-ever wild card by winning five straight games to close the regular season and beating the Packers 20–0 in the season finale.

Lem Barney had a 74-yard kick return to set up an Errol Mann field goal, a 65-yard punt return to set up Greg Landry's 13-yard touchdown pass to Charlie Sanders, and a 49-yard interception return for a touchdown. Fans stormed the field after the game and celebrated the Lions' first playoff appearance since their championship season of 1957 by tearing down the Tiger Stadium goalposts.

The Lions drew the Cowboys in the opening round of the playoffs. Had they lost to the Packers that day, they would have missed the postseason and the Rams (9–4–1) would have been the NFC's first wild card.

Lem Barney runs after intercepting a pass during the Lions' 31–28 victory over the Green Bay Packers on October 10, 1971 at Tiger Stadium in Detroit.
COURTESY OF GETTY IMAGES

DECEMBER 26, 1970

LIONS SHUT OUT IN PLAYOFF RETURN

DESPITE THEIR status as a wild card, the Lions entered the 1970 playoffs as one of the Super Bowl favorites. They won four times by double digits during their season-ending five-game winning streak, beat two playoff teams and two other wild-card contenders in the process, and had the highest-scoring offense in the NFL (24.8 points per game).

But in a December 26 game againsst the Cowboys at the Cotton Bowl, the Lions could not muster a single point in a 5–0 defeat that remains the lowest-scoring playoff game in NFL history. The Lions had three turnovers and seven first downs in the game, and they gave up a safety with 4:45 left that doomed their comeback hopes.

Trailing 3–0 after a goal-line stand, the Lions took possession at their own 2-yard line and managed one yard on two running plays. Greg Landry dropped back to pass on third-and-9 but was sandwiched by George Andrie and Jethro Pugh in the end zone for a safety.

Bill Munson replaced Landry on the Lions' final offensive possession and converted a fourth-and-10 with a 39-yard pass to Earl McCullouch. Three plays later, with the ball in field goal range but needing a touchdown to win, Munson threw a pass high over the middle that glanced off McCullouch's fingertips and into Mel Renfro's arms for a game-clinching interception.

The Lions lost to the Cowboys in their playoff return at the Cotton Bowl in 1970.
COURTESY OF WIKIMEDIA COMMONS

GODFATHER OF THE ZONE BLITZ GETS HIS START IN DETROIT

LONG BEFORE he was a trailblazing defensive coordinator, Dick LeBeau was a playmaking defensive back who made three Pro Bowls in 14 seasons with the Lions.

A fifth-round pick by the Browns in 1959, LeBeau signed with the Lions after he was cut in rookie camp and quickly became a staple in Detroit's star-studded secondary. He had three or more interceptions in 12 straight seasons from 1960 to 1971, led the NFC with nine picks in 1970, and started 171 consecutive games, most at right cornerback.

LeBeau played in the same secondary as Hall of Famers Yale Lary, Night Train Lane, and Lem Barney, and he was enshrined in Canton himself in 2010. He finished his career with 62 interceptions, third all-time at the time of his retirement, and he spent 35 more seasons as an NFL coach, primarily with the Cincinnati Bengals and Pittsburgh Steelers, where he made five Super Bowls, won two championships, and helped popularize the zone blitz that's a fixture of NFL defenses today.

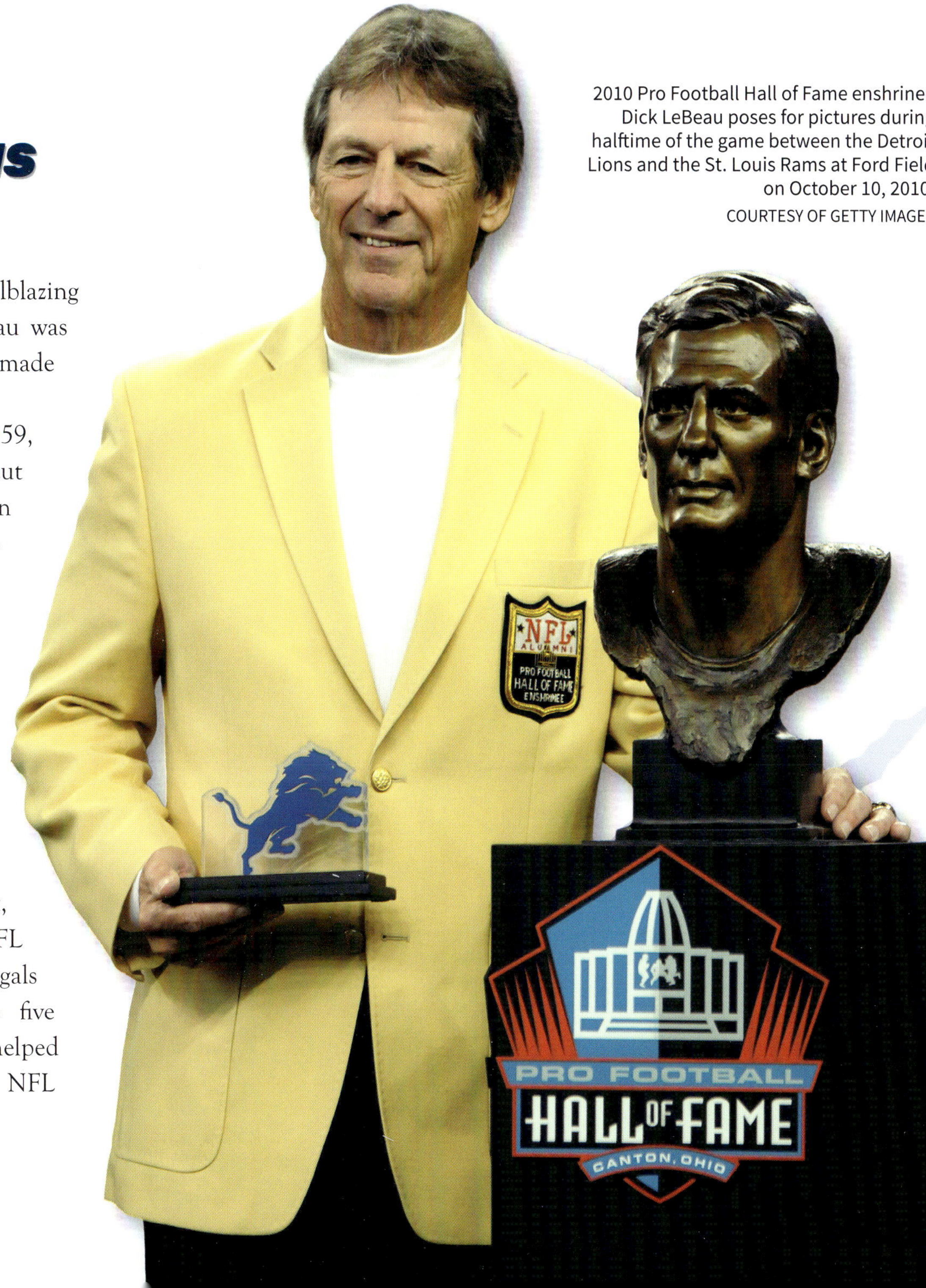

2010 Pro Football Hall of Fame enshrinee Dick LeBeau poses for pictures during halftime of the game between the Detroit Lions and the St. Louis Rams at Ford Field on October 10, 2010.
COURTESY OF GETTY IMAGES

OCTOBER 24, 1971

TRAGEDY STRIKES AT TIGER STADIUM

LIONS WIDE receiver Chuck Hughes collapsed and died on the field October 24, 1971, with 62 seconds left in a 28–23 loss to the Bears.

Hughes, 28, played sparingly in the 1971 season but entered the game in the fourth quarter as an injury replacement for Larry Walton. He caught a 32-yard pass on the Lions' final possession, and a few plays later ran a third-down route from his right flanker position over the middle of the field.

Greg Landry threw incomplete to Charlie Sanders on the play, and as Hughes turned and trotted back to the huddle he grabbed at his chest and fell face-first to the ground. Bears linebacker Dick Butkus began frantically waving toward the Lions sideline, and team physicians Dr. Edwin Guise and Dr. Richard A. Thompson ran onto the field to attempt life-saving measures.

Guise administered mouth-to-mouth resuscitation while Thompson performed compressions on Hughes' chest. Lions trainer Kent Falb and a third doctor attending the game as a fan helped load Hughes onto a stretcher.

A wiry Texan who was known for wearing cowboy boots and Stetson hats, Hughes's arms fell limp by his side as he was rolled toward a waiting ambulance. He was pronounced dead at 4:41 p.m. at Henry Ford Hospital.

Lions players wept openly in the locker room after the game, and the entire team and a contingent of Bears players attended Hughes's funeral two days later. Alex Karras, who had retired one season earlier, wrote a guest column in the *Free Press* saying Hughes hurt his chest in a preseason game and "never did feel good after that." Doctors said Hughes died of a heart attack stemming from an artery clogged by blood clots that was not related to his preseason injury.

Hughes is believed to be the only NFL player to die on the field, though at least two other NFL or AFL players died directly from injuries sustained during games.

Wide receiver Chuck Hughes lies on the field at Tiger Stadium, as the Chicago Bears' Dick Butkus and officials await assistance. Hughes died within the hour at Henry Ford Hospital of a heart attack.
COURTESY OF GETTY IMAGES

JULY 18, 1974

REMEMBERING DON McCAFFERTY

NEARLY THREE years after Chuck Hughes died on the field, the Lions lost another member of their organization unexpectedly. Head coach Don McCafferty, who replaced Joe Schmidt after the 1972 season, suffered a heart attack while doing yard work at his West Bloomfield home and died July 28, 1974, at the start of training camp.

McCafferty, 53, had passed a routine physical earlier that spring and was a day removed from leading the Lions through their first public scrimmage of summer. Lions veterans were on strike at the time and were meeting at the Pontiac Sheraton hotel when they heard news of McCafferty's passing across the street at Pontiac St. Joseph Mercy Hospital.

In a surprise move, the Lions named Rick Forzano interim coach over defensive line coach Ed Khayat and defensive backs coach Bob Hollway. Forzano was an assistant on the same staff as McCafferty at Kent State and had college head-coaching experience at UConn and Navy.

The Lions went 7–7 in Forzano's first season as head coach and again in 1975. He resigned early in the 1976 season after a 1–3 start and was replaced by Tommy Hudspeth.

Head coach Rick Forzano celebrates the Lions' 28–17 win over the San Francisco 49ers at Candlestick Park on November 2, 1975.
COURTESY OF GETTY IMAGES

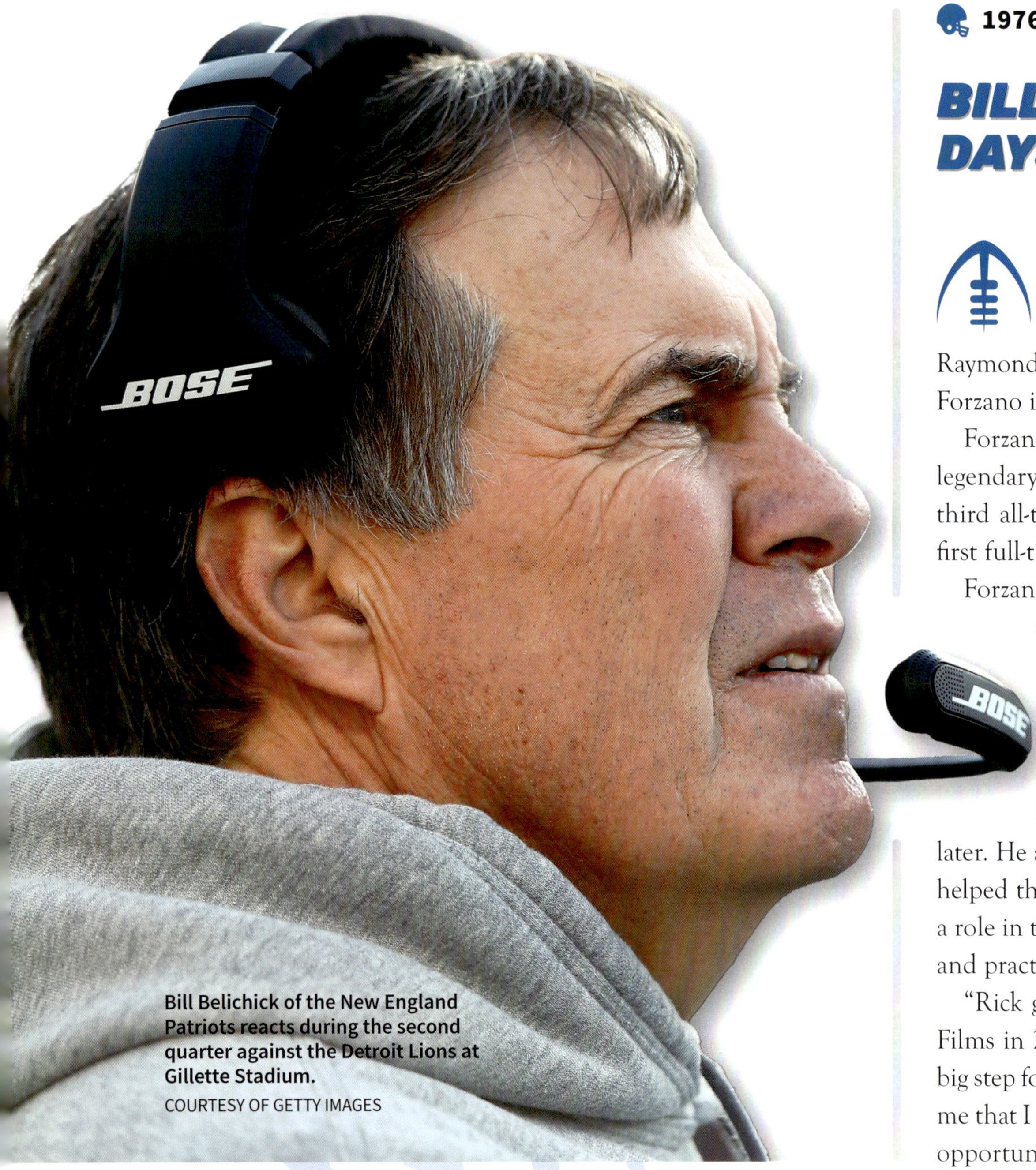

Bill Belichick of the New England Patriots reacts during the second quarter against the Detroit Lions at Gillette Stadium.
COURTESY OF GETTY IMAGES

1976

BILL BELICHICK'S EARLY DAYS IN DETROIT

THERE WAS nothing remarkable about Rick Forzano's tenure as head coach, except for maybe the staff he employed: future NFL head coaches Jerry Glanville, Raymond Berry, Joe Bugel, and Bill Belichick all worked under Forzano in Detroit.

Forzano hired Bugel and Belichick and gave Belichick, the legendary former New England Patriots head coach who ranks third all-time in the NFL with 302 regular-season victories, his first full-time job as an assistant in 1976.

Forzano briefly lived with Belichick's family after joining Navy as an assistant, where he worked with Belichick's father, Steve, and had a young Bill break down film for him at 10 years old.

Belichick entered the NFL as a special assistant with the Baltimore Colts in 1975 before joining the Lions as a 23-year-old special teams assistant a year later. He also coached receivers and tight ends in Detroit, and he helped the Lions evolve their video department when he played a role in the hire of Quinn Palamides to videotape training camp and practices.

"Rick gave me a great opportunity here," Belichick told NFL Films in 2017. "The opportunity to coach a position is, that's a big step for any coach. And that was an opportunity that Rick gave me that I probably wasn't ready for, but I certainly appreciated the opportunity for it."

1968–1977

A REVOLUTIONARY TIGHT END

ONE OF the players Bill Belichick worked directly with during his time in Detroit was Hall of Fame tight end Charlie Sanders.

A basketball and football star at the University of Minnesota, Sanders used his soft hands and leaping ability to help revolutionize the position as one of the best pass-catching tight ends of his era. He played 10 seasons for the Lions (1968–77), made seven Pro Bowls, and was named to the NFL's all-decade team of the 1970s.

Sanders had six seasons with at least 500 yards receiving and retired after the 1977 season as the franchise's all-time leader with 336 catches. In 1976, before suffering a knee injury that curtailed his playing career, he teamed with David Hill as Belichick helped the Lions pioneer the two-tight-end offense. Sanders and Hill played frequently together that season and combined for 10 of the Lions' 20 touchdowns.

Dubbed "The Ultimate Lion" by Dave Bing, Sanders spent 43 years with the organization before his passing in 2015. He worked as a broadcaster, assistant coach, and member of the personnel department.

Tight end Charlie Sanders makes a catch during the Lions' 24–13 loss to the St. Louis Cardinals on December 21, 1975, in Detroit.
COURTESY OF GETTY IMAGES

1976 aeriel shot
of the Pontiac Silverdome
COURTESY OF GETTY IMAGES

AUGUST 22, 1975

THE PONTIAC SILVERDOME OPENS

THE LIONS spent their first 40 years as a franchise playing in the city of Detroit, but in 1975 they moved about 30 miles north of downtown to the suburb of Pontiac.

Both the Lions and Tigers asked for help building new stadiums in 1968, and the city of Pontiac offered a 199-acre tract of land owned by the city's school board that September. Dearborn, Walled Lake, and Southfield also had interest in bringing the Lions to town, but their proposals fell by the wayside for various reasons, and the Lions settled on Pontiac after a disagreement with the city of Detroit on where to build a stadium. The city wanted to use a small parcel of waterfront land near Cobo Hall, while the Lions favored a larger plot by the Michigan State Fairgrounds on the northern 8 Mile border of the city.

On August 22, 1975, Pontiac Metropolitan Stadium opened for a preseason game against the Chiefs despite still being under construction. Later known as the Pontiac Silverdome, the $55.7 million domed stadium was roofless for the entire preseason, and heavy rainstorms in the days leading up to the opener left so much water in the facility that helicopters had to be used to dry the field.

Hot dogs cost 65 cents, beer was 70 cents, the stadium seated 80,000 people, and the Lions rallied for a 27–24 win over the Chiefs with the building at three-quarters capacity.

The Teflon-coated fiberglass roof was completed before the regular season home opener October 6 against the Cowboys, a 36–10 defeat, and the stadium was for a time the world's largest air-supported domed structure.

The Lions played 27 seasons at the Silverdome, from 1975 to 2001, and the building hosted Super Bowl XVI, WrestleMania III, a World Cup soccer game, the NBA's Detroit Pistons, and the NCAA Basketball Tournament.

NOVEMBER 25, 1976

THE JUICE GETS LOOSE ON THANKSGIVING

O. J. SIMPSON tied the NFL single-game rushing record of 250 yards in 1973 and broke it three years later against the Lions in a memorable performance on Thanksgiving Day.

Simpson ran for 273 yards and two touchdowns on 29 carries in the Lions' 27–14 win over the Buffalo Bills. He scored on runs of 48 and 12 yards in the second half, but the Lions scored the game's first 20 points to snap a three-game Thanksgiving losing streak.

"He is in a class by himself, and there is no doubt about that," Tommy Hudspeth told the *Free Press* after the game. "What more can you say about him? He is just one hellacious football player."

Dexter Bussey ran for 137 yards and Greg Landry threw two touchdown passes for the Lions, but officials stopped the game when Simpson broke the rushing record in the second half and the Silverdome crowd saluted him with a rousing ovation.

Simpson's 273 yards remains the sixth-highest single-game total in NFL history. The Lions' Bob Hoernschemeyer is second on the Thanksgiving rushing list with a 198-yard performance (including a 96-yard touchdown) in a 1950 win over the Yanks.

The Bills' O. J. Simpson waits for teammate Joe DeLamielleure to move into blocking position before trying to run past the Lions' Levi Johnson. Simpson rushed for 273 yards, but it was not enough as Detroit beat Buffalo, 27–14.
COURTESY OF GETTY IMAGES

APRIL 29, 1980

BILLY BALL COMES TO DETROIT

THE LIONS went seven straight seasons without a winning record from 1973 to 1979, and after going 2–14 to close the decade earned the first pick in the 1980 draft, where the prize was Oklahoma running back Billy Sims.

The Lions and Sims spent six contentious weeks trying to negotiate a contract before the draft. Sims wanted $4.5 million, the Lions offered $700,000, and when the two sides remained far apart with the draft approaching, Sims's agent, Jerry Argovitz, threatened to take his Heisman Trophy winner to the CFL.

The Lions picked Sims anyway, and the two sides eventually agreed on a deal that paid Sims an estimated $2 million over four seasons, a record for a rookie. With his violent rushing style and wearing the Lions' iconic No. 20 jersey, Sims gained 1,303 yards and led the NFL with 13 rushing touchdowns as a rookie, and the Lions went 9–7 and immediately became contenders in the NFC.

"If I can stay healthy," Sims told the *Free Press* forebodingly on the day of his signing, "a lot of good things will happen."

Running back Billy Sims takes a handoff in a 23–7 win over the Chicago Bears on November 22, 1981, at Soldier Field.
COURTESY OF GETTY IMAGES

1980

"ANOTHER ONE BITES THE DUST"

NEARLY A DECADE after Lem Barney and Mel Farr earned gold records as backup vocalists for Marvin Gaye, another group of Lions found their way into the recording studio.

Jimmy "Spiderman" Allen, a veteran defensive back who won two Super Bowls with the Steelers before being traded to the Lions, heard the Queen song "Another One Bites the Dust" on his car stereo as he was driving to the airport for a preseason game against the Bengals in 1980.

Allen found the tune catchy, and when he heard other Lions singing it in the locker room, he adopted it as the team's theme song.

Jimmy "Spiderman" Allen, full-time defensive back and part-time recording artist for the Lions.
COURTESY OF THE DETROIT LIONS

With Sims lifting the Lions to a 4–0 start in the regular season, Allen, David Hill, and James Hunter cut their own version of the song with some Lions-centric changes to the lyrics:

Are you ready? Are you ready for this?
Are you sitting on the edge or your seat?
Come and watch the Detroit Lions
That no one seems to beat.

The Lions never made it to New Orleans for the Super Bowl, as the song promised, but the tune was a hit in Detroit.

1975–1985

DOUG ENGLISH RETIRES—THE FIRST TIME

BEFORE BILLY SIMS took the NFL by storm, the Lions were dealt a blow at the start of the 1980 season when Pro Bowl defensive tackle Doug English, the team's MVP in 1979, retired unexpectedly.

English did not report with veterans for the start of training camp that summer, and in early August sent head coach Monte Clark a letter postmarked from Glouchester, England, explaining his business interests had grown so large they would not allow him to properly commit to football anymore.

It was more than just a business decision. English, a second-round pick out of Texas in 1975, also was dealing with the physical toll of five years of football and the mental strain of playing for a perennial loser. In 1981 he returned to the team after a one-year hiatus.

In his final five seasons, English made three Pro Bowls and was selected first- or second-team All-Pro four times. He had 13 sacks and two safeties in 1983—his four career safeties are tied for the most by a defensive player in NFL history—and retired for good after suffering a neck injury that required surgery in 1985.

Doug English chases quarterback Vince Ferragamo of the Los Angeles Rams during a 1983 game in Anaheim. The Rams prevailed 21–10.
COURTESY OF GETTY IMAGES

REIGN OF THE SILVER RUSH

THE LIONS teetered between not very good and slightly above average for most of Doug English's 10 seasons over 11 years with the team, despite the presence of one of the NFL's most dominant defensive lines.

English, Al "Bubba" Baker, John Woodcock, and Dave Pureifory comprised the original "Silver Rush," a group so fearsome it had its own football card in the 1980 Fleer set. English was the founding member of the group as a 1975 draft pick, but Baker took it to new heights when he showed up three years later as a second-round pick out of Colorado State.

Though sacks were not recognized officially at the time, Baker recorded 23 of them during his Rookie-of-the-Year campaign in 1978, and the Lions had a club record 55 as team.

Baker made three straight Pro Bowls to start his career. Woodcock found a home at defensive tackle after stints at linebacker and defensive end. Pureifory, a local star from Ecorse High and Eastern Michigan, was the team's Defensive MVP in 1980. And William Gay, who was drafted as a tight end by the Denver Broncos and traded to the Lions as a rookie, replaced Woodcock as a full-time starter in 1981 and had 60 sacks (15.5 of them unofficial) in his 10 seasons in Detroit.

Dave Pureifory in pursuit of the Chiefs' Joe Delaney during a 1981 game.
COURTESY OF GETTY IMAGES

NOVEMBER 27, 1980

A THANKSGIVING "NIGHTMARE"

THE LIONS would have made the playoffs in 1980 if not for a stunning Thanksgiving loss to the Bears in what was for a time the shortest overtime game in NFL history.

Bears running back Dave Williams returned the overtime kickoff 95 yards for a touchdown as the Bears rallied from 14 points down in the fourth quarter for a 23–17 win.

Williams fielded Eddie Murray's kickoff at the 5-yard line just outside the right hash, ran past a diving Eddie Lewis at the 20-yard line, then cut across field and raced down the left sideline for an easy touchdown on a play that took 21 seconds.

Monte Clark called it "probably the most disappointing, bitter loss I've ever experienced," and told UPI, "it was like a nightmare" watching Williams return the kick down the Lions sideline.

The Bears trailed 17–3 entering the fourth quarter but tied the game when quarterback Vince Evans scrambled for a 4-yard touchdown with no time left on the final play of regulation. The Lions, who failed to convert two third-and-1s in the fourth quarter, finished the season 9–7 and tied the Vikings for first place in the NFC Central, but missed out on the playoffs due to the tiebreaker.

Bears quarterback Vince Evans takes a snap as Lions linebacker Stan White looks on.
COURTESY OF THE DETROIT LIONS

JANUARY 8, 1983

BACK IN THE PLAYOFFS, WITH AN ASTERISK

IN 1982, NFL teams played just nine games because of a player strike and resulting lockout that halted work for 57 days. The strike ended in early November, and with it came an agreement to expand the playoffs from eight to 16 teams and recast the postseason as the Super Bowl Tournament.

William Clay Ford called it "a Mickey Mouse playoff system and an asterisk season" in a story by the *Los Angeles Times*—and that was despite his team making the tournament as the last team in, in the NFC.

The Lions went 4–5 in the regular season and joined the Browns as the first teams in NFL history to qualify for the playoffs with losing records. They drew Washington in their tournament opener, lost 31–7, and did not look like they belonged on the same field.

The Lions committed five turnovers in the game and trailed, 24–0, at halftime. Billy Sims lost two fumbles, including one on the game's opening drive. Eric Hipple, who started at quarterback in place of the benched Gary Danielson, threw two interceptions (one was returned for a touchdown). And Alvin Garrett caught three touchdown passes for a Washington team that went on to win the Super Bowl.

Lions quarterback Eric Hipple throws a pass during the Lions' 31–7 loss to Washington in the first round of the 1982 playoffs.
COURTESY OF GETTY IMAGES

JULY 18, 1983

BUBBA GETS HIS WISH

BUBBA BAKER had a dominant five-season run in Detroit, racking up 74 sacks in 67 games, and when he wasn't harassing opposing quarterbacks he spent much of his time butting heads with management over contractual issues.

After his Rookie-of-the-Year season, Baker negotiated an extension to his original three-year contract that landed him an extra signing bonus. A year later, after posting 16 sacks and making the Pro Bowl in his second season, he skipped five weeks of training camp while negotiating another extension and bonus.

After piling up 8.5 more sacks in the nine-game strike season of 1982, Baker told reporters he was done with the contract disputes. "We're going to walk in there like gentlemen and say, is it yes or no?" he told the *Free Press*. "If I don't get what I want, that's it. . . . I wouldn't play another down if I don't get it."

The Lions wouldn't give "it" to Baker, and on July 18, 1983, at the start of training camp, traded him to the St. Louis Cardinals for defensive tackle Mike Dawson and a draft choice.

Baker, 26 years old at the time of the trade, reunited with Floyd Peters, his first defensive line coach with the Lions, in St. Louis and posted three double-digit sack seasons in four years there before finishing his career with the Browns and Vikings.

Al Baker sacks quarterback Steve Bartkowski of the Atlanta Falcons during a 1980 game in Atlanta.
COURTESY OF GETTY IMAGES

DECEMBER 18, 1983

LIONS CLINCH FIRST DIVISION TITLE IN 26 YEARS

THE LIONS were 5–6 when they played the Packers in Week 12 of the 1983 season at Milwaukee County Stadium, and their chances of winning their first division title in 26 years seemed bleak when they fell behind 20–3 at halftime.

But Billy Sims ran for a career-high 189 yards as the Lions rallied to send the game to overtime, and Eddie Murray atoned for a missed 33-yard field goal at the start of the extra session when he hit the game-winner from 37 yards out three plays after a Bobby Watkins interception.

The Lions stunned the Steelers four days later, intercepting five passes in a 45–3 Thanksgiving victory, and when they beat the Vikings 13–2 the next week—with Minnesota's only points coming on a safety when punter Mike Black purposely stepped out of the back of the end zone—they were well on their way to their first division title since 1957.

The Lions lost a road game to the Bengals in Week 15 but had a playoff berth wrapped up by the time they took the field for their regular season finale, a 23–20 win over the Buccaneers that was accompanied by bad news: Eric Hipple injured his thumb and would not be available for the Lions' playoff game two weeks later against the 49ers.

Jimmy Williams (59) and William Graham (33) of the Lions battle for possesion of the ball against Eric Dickerson of the Los Angeles Rams during a game at Anaheim Stadium on October 2, 1983.
COURTESY OF GETTY IMAGES

DECEMBER 31, 1983

A MISS AND A PRAYER

AS EDDIE MURRAY lined up to kick the would-be game-winning field goal with 11 seconds left in the Lions' New Year's Eve playoff game against the 49ers, TV cameras panned to Monte Clark on the sideline and found the Lions coach clasping his hands in prayer.

Clark, wearing a Honolulu blue sweater with silver and white stripes on the sleeves and his name emblazoned on the left breast, cupped his hands over his face and closed his eyes, then opened them just in time to see Murray's 43-yard kick sail wide right.

"I was trying to guide it, to make sure I didn't miss it. And I led it too far to the right," Murray told the *Free Press* after the game. "It was a foolish thing I did. I should have done the normal thing I always do—kick the stuff out of it."

While the game always will be remembered for Murray's miss and Clark's devotion denied, there were plenty of contributing factors to the loss.

Billy Sims carries the ball against the 49ers in a 1983 playoff game.
COURTESY OF THE DETROIT LIONS

Gary Danielson, playing in place of the injured Eric Hipple, threw five interceptions that led to 17 San Francisco points, and Joe Montana was his usual clutch self with the game on the line. Montana completed all six of his passes on the 49ers' go-ahead touchdown drive and threaded a 14-yard pass to Freddie Solomon for the game-winning score with 1:23 to play.

Billy Sims ran for 114 yards and two scores, and Murray made a then-playoff-record 54-yard field goal just before halftime, but the loss sent the Lions into a tailspin it took years to recover from. They didn't win more than seven games in a season the rest of the decade and didn't make the playoffs again until there was a new No. 20 in town.

OCTOBER 21, 1984

SIMS'S CAREER CUT SHORT

BILLY SIMS BROKE teammate Dexter Bussey's franchise rushing record on his first carry of an October 21, 1984, game against the Minnesota Vikings—and saw his career come to a crashing and unexpected halt 21 carries later when he suffered a devastating knee injury.

Sims was injured on a sweep right when he planted to cut upfield and his foot stuck in the Metrodome turf as Vikings linebacker Walker Lee Ashley hit him around the shoulders.

"I remember seeing it like it happened yesterday," Eddie Murray said in a 2015 interview. "It was just like you just rotated around his knee and the bottom half of his leg just stayed planted in the ground and his body twisted around his knee."

Sims suffered multiple ligament injuries on the play and shattered the bearing surface of his knee joint. He underwent seven hours of surgery the next day, and though he vowed to return in a news conference the day after his surgery, he never played another down of football.

Twenty-one months later, just shy of his 31st birthday, Sims announced his retirement from the NFL.

Sims finished his Lions career with 5,106 yards rushing, still the second most in franchise history. He topped 1,000 yards in three of his first four seasons, with the lone exception being in the strike-shortened year of 1982, and was on pace to do so again at the time of his injury. He made three straight Pro Bowls to start his career and was a two-time second-team All-Pro selection. And if not for the injury, Sims said in 2015, "I think I might have had a chance to get in the Hall of Fame."

"Not bragging, just even 4½ years, over 5,100 yards is pretty good," he said. "I was on a good pace, I had a good supporting cast of guys, we was more of a run team anyway, and might have had a shot."

Running back Billy Sims while on the bench during a 1984 preseason game against the Buffalo Bills.
COURTESY OF GETTY IMAGES

DECEMBER 19, 1984

UNLUCKY NO. 7

MONTE CLARK, who played for Tom Landry and worked under Don Shula, replaced Tommy Hudspeth as Lions coach in 1978 and spent seven years on the job—more than any Lions coach to that point except George Wilson.

He had two winning seasons, in 1980 and 1983, and a 43-61-1 career record, but the Lions went into a tailspin after Sims's injury, losing six of their final eight games, and William Clay Ford announced in a two-paragraph statement he had fired Clark on December 19, 1984.

Clark, who was given personnel control over Russ Thomas when he was hired, replaced popular quarterback Greg Landry with Gary Danielson in one of his first moves as coach and was around for the duration of Sims's shooting star of a career. He was a football man of high integrity, but he never got the buy-in he needed from players and did not have the charisma to lead a turnaround.

Seven weeks after they fired Clark, the Lions hired Arizona State coach Darryl Rogers as his replacement. Rogers got off to an inauspicious start with the Lions, telling an Arizona radio station on the day he was hired he didn't know much about the team because he had spent his entire 20-plus-year coaching career in college.

Head coach Monte Clark looks on from the sidelines during a game circa 1982.
COURTESY OF GETTY IMAGES

APRIL 30, 1985

TWO LINEMEN AND A RUSTED HOOPTIE

IN DARRYL ROGERS'S first draft as head coach, the Lions landed two players who would go on to be anchors of their offensive line for more than a decade, Lomas Brown and Kevin Glover.

Brown, a left tackle out of Florida, made six Pro Bowls in 11 seasons with the Lions and was inducted into the Pride of the Lions ring of honor in 2023. He said he never heard from anyone associated with the team in the buildup to the draft and was stunned when Rogers called to tell him he'd be the No. 6 pick.

He flew to Detroit the next day and was shuttled to the Silverdome for his introductory news conference in an equipment staffer's car.

"It was rusted out at the bottom," Brown recalled. "I forgot what make and model it was, but it was a hooptie. And I'm like. 'Oh my God.' I'm saying to myself, 'Man, I'm the sixth pick in the draft and they send a one-armed equipment guy to come pick me up in this hooptie, man.' And I'm telling you, I froze from that. Cause again, it was rusted out at the bottom. I froze from the airport all the way out to the Pontiac Silverdome, and that was my first experience with the Lions."

In Round 2, the Lions took Glover, a first-team All-American at Maryland, with the No. 34 overall pick. Glover made 161 starts in 13 seasons in Detroit. He played both guard spots early in his career and made the Pro Bowl his last three years with the Lions at center.

Both Brown and Glover spent the second halves of their careers in Detroit blocking for Hall of Fame running back Barry Sanders.

Kevin Glover (53) and Lomas Brown block the Green Bay Packers' Tony Bennett (90).
COURTESY OF GETTY IMAGES

Quarterback Andre Ware listens to head coach Wayne Fontes on the sideline during a 1993 game against the Phoenix Cardinals.
COURTESY OF GETTY IMAGES

1986–1993

A QUARTERBACK BUST (TIMES TWO)

THE LIONS went 43 years between Pro Bowl quarterbacks, from Greg Landry in 1971 to Matthew Stafford in 2014, but it wasn't for a lack of trying.

Gary Danielson and Eric Hipple rotated as starters for most of the first half of the 1980s, until the Lions went looking for a long-term solution at the position and took Heisman Trophy runner-up Chuck Long with the 12th pick of the 1986 draft.

Long went 4–17 as starter in five seasons in Detroit. He threw more interceptions (28) than touchdowns (19) and was traded to the Rams in 1990—after the Lions spent another first-round pick on quarterback Andre Ware, the run-and-shoot gunslinger from Houston.

Ware, the seventh pick of the draft, was an even bigger bust than Long, making six starts in four seasons in Detroit and completing 51.6% of his passes. The Lions scrapped the run-and-shoot offense not long after Ware came to town, and Ware never took to a more conventional NFL offense nor got much of an opportunity to play behind Rodney Peete and Erik Kramer—who had their own timeshare at the position until the Lions dipped their toes into the free-agent quarterback waters in 1994.

OCTOBER 20, 1988

THE TROUBLED LIFE OF REGGIE ROGERS

REGGIE ROGERS, the No. 7 pick of the 1987 draft, had his career cut short under tragic circumstances.

Rogers played in only six games as a rookie after he spent time at a counseling center for what he and his mother said were emotional problems. Rogers's brother, Don, died of a drug overdose in 1986, and his sister, Jackie, went missing for five days from his suburban Detroit home, leaving him on the verge of a nervous breakdown.

In 1988, Rogers was charged with three counts of voluntary manslaughter after he ran a red light and struck an oncoming vehicle, killing three teens. Rogers was driving 60 mph in a 35-mph zone and had a blood alcohol content of 0.15, above the legal limit, according to UPI.

Rogers, who broke two vertebrae in his neck in the crash, was convicted on reduced charges of negligent homicide in December of 1989 and spent nearly 13 months in prison. He had one sack in 11 games with the Lions before his release, appeared in games with the Buffalo Bills and Tampa Bay Buccaneers during his comeback attempt, and died in 2013 at the age of 49 because of cocaine and alcohol intoxication, according to the *Seattle Times*.

Reggie Rogers brings down Atlanta Falcons running back Gerald Riggs.
COURTESY OF THE DETROIT LIONS

1988–1995

CHRIS SPIELMAN, TOUGHNESS PERSONIFIED

NO LIONS player better embodied Detroit's blue-collar toughness than Chris Spielman.

A second-round pick out of Ohio State in 1988, Spielman missed four games in eight seasons with the team and topped 100 tackles every year. He played without regard for his body, launching himself at opposing ball carries, and was legendary for his maniacal workout routines and film habits. Just 6 feet tall and with a 4.86-second 40-yard dash, Spielman made up for his comparatively average athleticism with instincts, intensity, and leadership few could match. "My approach is to win at all cost," he told the *Free Press* after the draft. "All he wanted to do was play football and knock you down," Lions coach Wayne Fontes told NFL Films.

Spielman finished second in Defensive Rookie of the Year voting and made four Pro Bowls in Detroit. He played two seasons for the Buffalo Bills before a neck injury ended his career. He returned to Detroit in a front office role in December of 2020, where he helped run the coaching and GM searches that landed Dan Campbell and Brad Holmes and also helped with scouting, coaching, and culture building.

Chris Spielman anchored the Lions' defense.
COURTESY OF GETTY IMAGES

SEPTEMBER 19, 1988

"MAYDAY" GOES UNANSWERED

LONG-TIME *Free Press* columnist George Puscas called it "the dumbest play" in what to that point was the 55-year history of the Lions.

On September 19, 1988, the Lions gave away a game to the Saints when they failed to convert a fake punt on fourth-and-18 from their own 12-yard line late in the third quarter of a game they led by two points. Lions punter Jim Arnold threw the pass from his own end zone to gunner Carl Painter, who never looked up for the ball.

Arnold explained after the game he did "what I've been trained to do and coached to do." The Lions had an automatic audible for their punt team, where Arnold was to throw to an uncovered gunner if one of four players—the punter, personal protector, or either gunner—called "Mayday."

Painter, however, was a rookie filling in at gunner as an injury replacement and no one could say for certain whether the "Mayday" call came from the Lions bench or a Saints player on the field.

The pass fell incomplete, Dalton Hilliard scored two plays later on a 3-yard run, and the Saints went on to win, 22–14.

Jim Arnold averaged 42.7 yards per punt in eight seasons with the Lions.
COURTESY OF GETTY IMAGES

NOVEMBER 13, 1988

ASK AND YOU SHALL RECEIVE

DARRYL ROGERS was considered an offensive innovator when the Lions hired him as head coach in 1985, but his star quickly faded after back-to-back losing seasons to start his tenure in Detroit.

The Lions dropped six of their final eight games to finish 7–9 in 1985 and slipped to 5–11 the following year. Near the end of a 4–12 campaign in 1987, with rumors circulating that Rogers was on the hot seat, William Clay Ford told a small group of reporters at a late-season practice he planned to bring Rogers back as head coach.

That decision prompted one of the most memorable lines a Lions coach has ever uttered. Told of Ford's plans, Rogers, appreciative of his boss's loyalty, joked, "What does a guy have to do to get fired around here?"

Before the 1988 season was over, he would find out. A soft-spoken coach with an underwhelming staff whose tenure was marred by poor draft picks (Chuck Long and Reggie Rogers) and player distrust, Rogers went 18–40 with the Lions and was replaced by Wayne Fontes, his defensive coordinator, with five weeks left in the season.

Head coach Darryl Rogers looks on as a player and official talk during a 1986 game against the Pittsburgh Steelers.
COURTESY OF GETTY IMAGES

DECEMBER 22, 1988

FONTES HIRED FULL-TIME

THE LIONS closed the 1988 season with two wins over the Packers in their final five games and a one-point road loss to the division-champion Bears, and that was enough to give the jovial Wayne Fontes the job full-time.

William Clay Ford never interviewed anyone else for the job, telling the *Free Press* he was impressed with how Fontes was able to re-energize a team that seemed to be going through the motions most of the year.

"He took a team that was probably as low as you can get and revitalized it," Ford said. "Wayne put a new spirit and a new life in them."

A football and baseball star at Michigan State, Fontes spent four seasons as Lions defensive coordinator before becoming head coach. He was gregarious and player-friendly, and when he was finally fired after the 1996 season, he left as the winningest and losingest coach in Lions history with a 67–71 record (.486).

Fontes is still the longest-tenured coach in franchise history, and the Lions made four playoff appearances and won two division titles in his eight full seasons with the team.

Head coach Wayne Fontes speaks during a press conference circa 1990s.
COURTESY OF GETTY IMAGES

1989

THE SILVER STRETCH COMES TO DETROIT

THE LIONS had one of the most boring, ineffective offenses in the NFL in 1988. They ranked last in the league in points scored, total yards, and plays run, and they managed a measly 20 offensive touchdowns in 16 games.

In one of his first moves as full-time head coach, Wayne Fontes, with a nudge from Russ Thomas, hired Darrel "Mouse" Davis as offensive coordinator.

Davis was the innovative offensive mind often credited with inventing the run-and-shoot offense, a spread concept that deployed four receivers and one running back in most sets and rarely used a tight end. Davis told *Sports Illustrated* in 1989 the Lions had only eight plays, but with a dozen or more options off each. The timing offense relied largely on quarterbacks and receivers reading the defense the same way.

Fontes dubbed the offense "The Silver Stretch," and Davis had flummoxed defenses with a version of it at every level of football. He coached in high school, college, the CFL, and the USFL before coming to the Lions, and though he lasted just two seasons in Detroit—Fontes decided to switch to a more traditional offense after the 1990 season—the Lions finished fifth in the league in scoring (despite ranking second-to-last in plays run) in his final season with the team.

Darrel "Mouse" Davis talks with quarterback Andre Ware at a Lions practice.
COURTESY OF THE DETROIT LIONS

APRIL 23, 1989

"WE'RE TAKING BARRY"

THE 1989 draft was one of the best of all time. Four Hall of Famers went in the first five picks, a fifth went later in the first round, and the Lions landed arguably the greatest running back in NFL history, Barry Sanders.

Sanders was coming off a Heisman Trophy–winning campaign at Oklahoma State, where he rushed for 2,628 yards and 37 touchdowns (and scored two more on returns) to set 34 NCAA records. He was electric and elusive, and when the Lions showed up to his pro day that spring, Wayne Fontes told the *Detroit News* he was so wowed by Sanders's performance—Sanders ran a 4.39-second 40-yard dash and had a 41.5-inch vertical jump after driving straight to the workout from the airport—he lit up a cigar as personnel men from other teams approached him about a trade.

"I pulled out the cigar and said, 'You guys can go home, we're taking Barry,'" Fontes said.

The third pick of the 1989 draft, Barry Sanders ran for 15,269 yards, the fourth most in NFL history.

COURTESY OF GETTY IMAGES

The Lions had the third pick in the draft. The Dallas Cowboys took UCLA quarterback Troy Aikman No. 1. The Green Bay Packers took mammoth Michigan State offensive tackle Tony Mandarich No. 2—Ron Hughes, the Lions' director of pro personnel at the time, said the Lions would have considered Mandarich had he been on the board—which left the Lion to choose between Sanders and Florida State cornerback Deion Sanders.

When Fontes introduced Barry Sanders at his post-draft news conference April 24, he gave the running back the same No. 20 jersey worn by Billy Sims, the Lions' last Heisman Trophy back, and Lem Barney, and chomped on another cigar.

"I told you people we were going to restore the roar," Fontes said, according to the *Free Press*. "He will electrify the crowd. . . . This guy is going to win some games for us."

DECEMBER 24, 1989

SANDERS SITS WITH RUSHING TITLE WITHIN REACH

BARRY SANDERS was a runaway winner for NFL Offensive Rookie of the Year, earning 69 of a possible 70 votes (with Indianapolis Colts receiver Andre Rison receiving the other).

He ran for 71 yards and a touchdown on nine carries in his debut against the Phoenix Cardinals days after signing his rookie contract, and finished the year with a then franchise-record 1,470 yards rushing—at the time the fourth most by a rookie in NFL history—and 14 touchdowns.

Sanders entered the last game of the regular season 70 yards behind Chiefs running back Christian Okoye for the NFL rushing title. Okoye ran for 98 yards in a win over the Miami Dolphins, while Sanders had 158 yards on 20 carries in a win over the Falcons, leaving him 10 yards short of Okoye's season total of 1,480 yards.

Sanders had just one carry after scoring his third touchdown of the game early in the fourth quarter and turned down a chance to reenter the game late to clinch the title.

"I just felt there was no need to play anymore," he explained to the *Free Press* after the game. "We already had won the game. Hopefully, it'll come in the future, but it didn't mean that much right now."

Barry Sanders looks on from the sidelines. He finished the 1989 season just 10 yards short of the rushing title.
COURTESY OF GETTY IMAGES

NOVEMBER 24, 1991

THUMBS UP, MIKE

BARRY SANDERS had four 200-yard rushing games in his career. The first, a 220-yard day against the Vikings, came under tragic circumstances on November 24, 1991, when guard Mike Utley suffered a paralyzing neck injury.

On the first play of the fourth quarter, Utley was in pass protection at right guard when Erik Kramer threw an 11-yard touchdown to Robert Clark. Rams lineman David Rocker jumped to try and block the pass and landed on Utley's neck when he came down, driving Utley's head into the Silverdome turf.

Utley lay motionless for several minutes while being tended to by trainers. He flashed a "thumbs-up" sign with his right hand as he was wheeled off the field by stretcher, and underwent four hours of surgery the next day at Henry Ford Hospital.

In surgery, doctors opened a 1.5-inch incision in Utley's neck to remove pieces of a ruptured spinal disc, then used a piece of bone from his pelvis to fuse his sixth and seventh vertebrae. He suffered severe spinal cord bleeding and a shattered sixth vertebrae, and remains paralyzed from the chest down.

Mike Utley is tended to by medical personnel after he was injured against the Los Angeles Rams at the Pontiac Silverdome.
COURTESY OF GETTY IMAGES

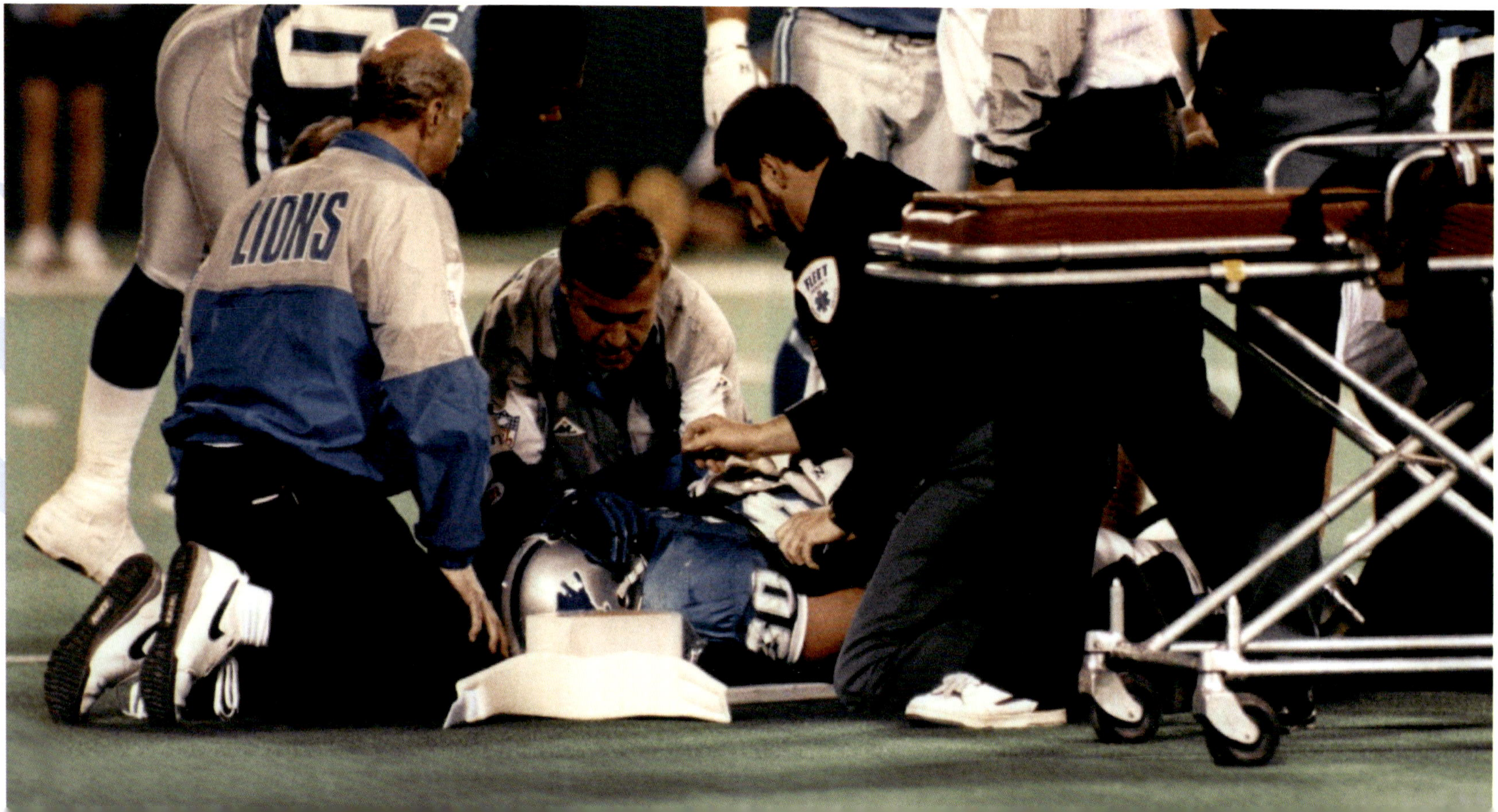

Lions tackle Lomas Brown is all smiles as he leaves the field following the Lions' 38-6 victory over the Dallas Cowboys in the 1991 NFC divisional playoff game.
COURTESY OF GETTY IMAGES

JANUARY 5, 1992

KRAMER LEADS LIONS TO FIRST PLAYOFF WIN IN 34 YEARS

WITH MIKE Utley's courage as inspiration, the Lions won their final six games of the 1991 regular season. They finished 12-4, won the NFC Central by one game over the Bears, and earned a date with the Cowboys in their first home playoff game since winning the 1957 championship.

In what was supposed to be a showcase of two of the NFL's great running backs, Barry Sanders and Emmitt Smith, Erik Kramer stole the show. The journeyman quarterback completed 29 of 38 passes for 341 yards and three touchdowns as the Lions cruised to a 38-6 victory.

"I didn't think Kramer had it in him," Cowboys linebacker Jack Del Rio told the *Free Press* after the game. "But they had enough confidence to give it to him and he responded. He had a hell of a game."

With the Cowboys focused on stopping Sanders, the Lions passed on all 14 of their first-down plays in the first half. Sanders did have a memorable 47-yard touchdown run in the fourth quarter, bouncing off one defender and turning around Tony Casillas on his way to the end zone, but he gained just 22 yards on his other 11 carries as the Lions advanced to their first NFC championship game.

JANUARY 12, 1992

PUNCHED IN THE MOUTH IN A PLAYOFF REMATCH

THE LIONS had a humbling start to the 1991 season, losing at Washington, 45–0, in a game Barry Sanders missed because of a rib injury. After the game, Wayne Fontes gathered his players in the middle of the locker room and told them to look around because "we'll be back here in December to play these guys to go to the Super Bowl."

The game was on January 12, not in December, but Fontes's premonition came true. The Lions got their rematch with Washington in the NFC title game—and were overwhelmed in another blowout, 41–10.

Sanders had 11 carries for 44 yards and the Lions committed three turnovers on offense. Erik Kramer fumbled on the second play from scrimmage, Darrell Green returned an Andre Ware interception for a touchdown, and Mark Rypien had a near-perfect passer rating as Washington outscored the Lions 24–0 in the second half.

"They're the better team," Chris Spielman told the *Free Press* after the game. "That's hard for me to face. But it's true and I know it."

Washington went on to win the Super Bowl, but not before Ford and Fontes shared a moment outside the stadium as snow fell after the game.

"I looked at him and I looked at his wife and I said, 'Mr. Ford, I'm very sorry and disappointed that we couldn't win this one for you,'" Fontes said in a 2013 interview. "And he and his wife looked at me both and said, 'That's OK. This is the farthest we've ever come and we're very proud of the team.'"

Cornerback Darrell Green (28) runs an interception back for touchdown during Washington's win over the Lions in the NFC championship game.
COURTESY OF GETTY IMAGES

APRIL 26, 1992

NOT JUST ANY KICKER

THE LIONS made the unusual decision to take a kicker in the second round of the 1992 draft, trading up for Washington State's Jason Hanson at Pick No. 56 overall.

The pick was a head-scratcher at the time. Hanson was All-Pac-10 as both a kicker and punter as a junior, but made just 10 of 22 field goals (with three kicks blocked) his senior season, and specialists rarely go that high in the draft.

But Hanson turned out to be the cherry on top of a solid draft that also included Robert Porcher and Tracy Scroggins. He kicked 19 game-winning field goals, including nine in overtime, in his 21-year career and he retired at age 42 in 2013 with NFL records for most 50-yard field goals (52) and most games played with one team (327).

Hanson finished with 495 field goals and 2,150 points, both third in the league at the time of his retirement, and was selected to the Lions' all-time team.

Jason Hanson attempts a kick against the Tampa Bay Buccaneers.
COURTESY OF GETTY IMAGES

JUNE 23, 1992

"WHEN ERIC PASSED, A PIECE OF ME DIED, TOO"

NEARLY SEVEN months to the day Mike Utley was paralyzed on the field, the Lions were dealt another tragic blow to their offensive line. Left guard Eric Andolsek was killed June 23, 1992, when he was hit by a truck while doing yardwork at his Thibodaux, Louisiana, home.

Andolsek was using the weed trimmer on his lawn at about 1 p.m. when the driver of the truck, the cab of an 18-wheeler without a trailer, fell asleep at the wheel. The truck went about 400 feet after striking Andolsek. Lomas Brown said blood was still visible on the freshly cut grass when players went to the funeral two days later.

Known for his toughness and tenacity and nicknamed "Table" because of the size of his back and shoulders, Andolsek was "quickly developing as being the best lineman on the team," Brown said in a 2024 interview.

Roughly 75 Lions attended Andolsek's funeral, including Brown, Rodney Peete, and the entire coaching staff. Chris Spielman delivered the eulogy, telling a packed chapel, "When Eric passed, a piece of me died, too." And on the field, the Lions offensive line struggled with two new starting guards in 1992.

The death of offensive lineman Eric Andolsek devastated the team.
COURTESY OF GETTY IMAGES

JANUARY 8, 1994

ALONE IN THE END ZONE

THE LIONS slumped to 5–11 in 1992, but rebounded to win their second division title in three years in the last game of the 1993 season, when they beat the Packers at the Silverdome 30–20 to set up a playoff rematch one week later.

Six days after throwing four interceptions in the division clincher, Hall of Fame quarterback Brett Favre led the Packers to a 28–24 wild-card upset, throwing for 204 yards and three touchdowns—all to Sterling Sharpe. The game-winner came with 55 seconds left, when Favre scrambled to his left and found Sharpe down the right sideline alone in the end zone against a busted coverage by Kevin Scott and William White for an easy 40-yard touchdown.

"That was kind of like the season has gone all year," Favre told the *Milwaukee Journal Sentinel*. "Just kind of, I don't want to say a hope and a prayer, but that's what it was."

Barry Sanders had a career playoff-high 169 yards rushing in his return from a knee injury, but Erik Kramer had another disappointing playoff showing with two interceptions, including one late in the third quarter that George Teague returned 101 yards for a game-changing touchdown.

After the game, Wayne Fontes insisted Kramer would be the Lions' starting quarterback again in 1994, telling the *News* it was a done deal "unless Dan Marino pops up, or somebody of that nature."

The Green Bay Packers' Sterling Sharpe scores the winning touchdown against the Lions in an NFC playoff game.
COURTESY OF GETTY IMAGES

MARCH 7, 1994

SCOTT MITCHELL THE SAVIOR

DAN MARINO NEVER did become available, returning to the Dolphins after his 1993 season was cut short by a torn Achilles. But his backup did.

On March 7, 1994, the Lions signed Scott Mitchell to be their new starting quarterback. Mitchell went 3–4 in seven starts with the Dolphins after Marino's injury, throwing for 1,773 yards and 12 touchdowns with eight interceptions.

The Lions, desperate for a savior at quarterback, gave Mitchell a three-year contract worth $11.1 million. The deal included a $5 million signing bonus, the second largest in NFL history at the time.

Scott Mitchell talks with coaches in a 1995 game against the Packers in Green Bay.
COURTESY OF GETTY IMAGES

"This guy, hopefully, is the missing piece that will one day take the Detroit Lions to the Super Bowl," Wayne Fontes said at Mitchell's introductory news conference, according to the *Free Press*.

A lefty who went 86 picks after Andre Ware in the 1990 draft, Mitchell played five productive but underwhelming seasons in Detroit. He helped the Lions make three playoff appearances and set then-franchise records with 4,338 yards passing and 32 touchdowns in 1995, but he never quite meshed in the locker room and was benched for rookie Charlie Batch two games into the 1998 season after throwing two bad interceptions in an overtime loss to the Bengals.

Mitchell, who re-signed with the Lions as a free agent in 1997 and was traded two years later to the Baltimore Ravens, went 27–30 as Lions starter and still ranks third on the franchise's all-time passing list (12,647 yards) behind Matthew Stafford and Bobby Layne. He said in social media posts in 2023 he feels unfairly blamed for the team's lack of playoff success, something Fontes hinted at in a conversation captured in the documentary *Bye Bye Barry*, when he told Sanders the team had everything to be successful "but the quarterback."

NOVEMBER 13, 1994

BARRY'S BEST DAY

THE MOST iconic performance of Barry Sanders's Hall of Fame career didn't look like anything special early on.

Sanders had 10 carries for 37 yards in the first half of a November 13, 1994, game against the Buccaneers, then exploded for 200 yards on 16 rushes after halftime. With Scott Mitchell out with a broken wrist, Sanders had electrifying runs of 23 and 69 yards to set up Lions touchdowns and a 48-yarder late in the fourth quarter to help clinch a 14–9 victory.

"God ain't made a better back in this lifetime," Wayne Fontes told the *Free Press* after the game.

Sanders had seven games with at least 120 yards rushing in the first 10 weeks of the 1994 season and left the Tampa game on pace to break Eric Dickerson's NFL record of 2,105 yards rushing. He fell short of that mark after pedestrian performances of 42 and 45 yards rushing the next two weeks, but finished the season with a league-best 1,883 yards. His 237 yards remains a franchise single-game record and one of the top 25 rushing performances in NFL history.

Barry Sanders seemed unstoppable in his 237-yard performance against the Tampa Bay Buccaneers.
COURTESY OF GETTY IMAGES

1994

MEL GRAY'S RECORD-SETTING SEASON

MEL GRAY started his career in the USFL and was one of pro football's best return men by the time he got to the Lions in 1989. Gray made four Pro Bowls in six seasons in Detroit and had one of the best seasons ever by a return specialist in 1994, when he returned three kicks for touchdowns.

Gray broke Ron Smith's NFL record for career return yardage (6,922 yards) on the opening kickoff of an October 23 win over the Bears. He fumbled at the end of that return but atoned for his mistake with a career-long 102-yard kick return later in the game.

Two weeks later, Gray returned a kick 91 yards for a touchdown in a loss to the Packers. Green Bay kicked away from Gray most of the day, but strayed from that plan after taking a 24–0 lead late in the first half. Gray fielded the kick at the 9-yard line and got a key block from Derrick Moore on his way to the end zone.

His final return touchdown of the season—and of his career—came December 17 in a win over the Vikings, when he took a kick back 98 yards for a score. The touchdown tied Ollie Matson's NFL record for most career return touchdowns (nine) and helped catapult the Lions into the playoffs.

A sign for kick/punt returner Mel Gray hanging from the stands during a 1994 game against the Minnesota Vikings.
COURTESY OF GETTY IMAGES

DECEMBER 31, 1994

ANOTHER PLAYOFF LOSS TO THE PACKERS

THE LIONS finished the 1994 season in a four-way tie for second place in the NFC Central and drew a first-round playoff rematch with the Packers at Lambeau Field. And a year after the best postseason performance of his career, Barry Sanders had his worst.

The Packers had little to worry about in the Lions' passing game with Scott Mitchell still out with a wrist injury, and they held Sanders to minus-1 yard rushing on 13 carries in a 16–12 victory. Green Bay's front seven dominated the line of scrimmage, and the Packers thwarted Sanders by moving Hall of Fame defensive lineman Reggie White all over the field.

"It's inconceivable," White told the *News* of Sanders's rushing total after the game. "I've seen this man do things I've never seen anyone do in my life."

The Packers scored on a fourth-and-goal play on the game's opening drive and led 10–0 at halftime. The Lions scored their only touchdown on a 3-yard Dave Krieg pass to Brett Perriman after a long Mel Gray kick return. They had a chance to win late in the game, but Herman Moore caught a pass out of bounds in the back of the end zone on the Lions' final offensive play, and the Packers took a safety as time expired for the final margin of victory.

Defensive end Reggie White puts pressure on quarterback Dave Krieg in a 1994 wild-card playoff game.
COURTESY OF GETTY IMAGES

1995

BIG BUCK BRINGS THE LIONS BACK TO LIFE

THE LIONS lost their first three games of the 1995 season, casting doubt on Wayne Fontes's future as head coach. Fontes compared himself to "that big buck that's in the field" at his news conference the day after a loss to the Arizona Cardinals, saying everyone was "trying to hunt him down, trying to shoot him. I just keep dodging those bullets. Everybody wants my rack on the wall."

The Lions upset the defending Super Bowl champion 49ers the next week, giving Fontes a temporary reprieve, but William Clay Ford turned the heat up on his coach's seat even more after the Lions fell to 3–6, telling the *Free Press* he "probably would" make a change if the Lions didn't make the playoffs.

With that ultimatum hanging over his head, the Big Buck engineered a miraculous second-half turnaround as the Lions closed the season with seven straight victories to earn a wild-card spot. They averaged 32.4 points per game over the final seven weeks and allowed more than 10 points just once after Thanksgiving to earn a date with the Eagles in the playoffs.

After taking over as head coach at the end of the 1988 season, Wayne Fontes kept the position until 1996.
COURTESY OF GETTY IMAGES

1995

HERMAN MOORE RACES INTO THE RECORD BOOKS

BARRY SANDERS had another 1,500-yard rushing season in 1995, his second of four straight, but he was far from the only star on the Lions offense.

Herman Moore and Brett Perriman set NFL records for catches (231) and yards (3,174) by teammates in a single season, and Moore broke Cris Carter's record with 123 catches on an astounding 206 targets for 1,686 yards.

The 10th pick out of Virginia in the 1991 draft, Moore was a champion college high jumper who blossomed into one of the NFL's best all-around receivers. He had rare size, strength, and leaping ability, and he overcame early-career drop problems to become a trusted playmaker downfield.

Moore caught 14 touchdowns in 1995, one shy of Cloyce Box's club record, and followed that up with two more 100-catch, 1,200-yard receiving seasons. A three-time first-team All-Pro selection, Moore played 11 of his 12 NFL seasons in Detroit and left in 2002 as the franchise leader in every major receiving category with 670 catches for 9,174 yards and 62 touchdowns. He remains the only receiver in franchise history with three straight 100-catch seasons.

Herman Moore played 11 seasons in Detroit and left as the franchise leader in every major receiving category.
COURTESY OF GETTY IMAGES

DECEMBER 30, 1995

A GUARANTEE GONE WRONG

THE LIONS closed the 1995 season on such a tear they were road favorites heading into their wild-card game against the Eagles. Asked about that anomaly during the week, Lomas Brown, the Lions' Pro Bowl left tackle, said that's how it should be.

"There is no question in my mind that we're going to win this game," he told the *Philadelphia Daily News*, via PhiladelphiaEagles.com. "It is just a matter of how much we are going to win it by and how long it is going to take."

Brown's comments served as bulletin-board material for the Eagles, who scored 38 first-half points on their way to a 58–37 victory. The Eagles led 38–7 at halftime and 51–7 in the third quarter. Rodney Peete, the ex-Lion, started at quarterback for the Eagles and threw three touchdown passes, including a 43-yard Hail Mary to Rob Carpenter at the end of the first half. And Philadelphia fans chanted Brown's name in jest as the game spiraled out of control.

The Lions finished the game with seven turnovers, and Wayne Fontes entered the 1996 season on the hot seat again.

Eagles running back Ricky Watters (32) carries the ball against the Lions in the NFC wild-card playoff game on December 30, 1995 at Veterans Stadium.
COURTESY OF GETTY IMAGES

JANUARY 13, 1997

A NEW GENERAL IN TOWN

WILLIAM CLAY Ford's patience with Wayne Fontes finally ran out at the end of a disastrous 1996 season. The Lions won four of their first six games, but Fontes pulled Scott Mitchell in the middle of a series in the second quarter of a Week 9 loss to the Giants, and Mitchell mocked his coach in a Halloween costume days later, wearing Mickey Mouse ears—Fontes was pictured in ears for a charitable promotion earlier in the season—and holding a cigar.

The Lions lost nine of their final 10 games, and Fontes was fired three days after the season on December 26.

"Don't feel sorry for me," Fontes said during a surprise appearance at the news conference to announce his firing, per the *Free Press*. "It's a chapter of my life that's over but I'll bleed Honolulu blue."

The Lions quickly zeroed in on Fontes's replacement when Bobby Ross resigned from the San Diego Chargers after losing a power struggle to general manager Bobby Beathard. Ross was a rigid disciplinarian who served in the Army, but he won a national championship in college at Georgia Tech and took the Chargers to the Super Bowl, and Ford was betting that his new coach's winning résumé would do wonders for the locker room.

The Lions brought in Bobby Ross after a poor showing in 1996.
COURTESY OF GETTY IMAGES

DECEMBER 21, 1997

BARRY TOPS 2,000 ON A SOMBER DAY

BARRY SANDERS reached the pinnacle of his remarkable career in 1997, when he joined Eric Dickerson and O. J. Simpson as the third back in NFL history to top 2,000 yards rushing.

After a slow start to the season with 53 yards in his first two games, Sanders finished with 14 straight 100-yard efforts and had 184 yards in a season-ending win over the New York Jets that sent the Lions to the playoffs.

The Jets held Sanders in check early, limiting him to 20 yards on his first eight carries. But Sanders broke a 47-yard run at the end of the third quarter and was closing in on history when he scored on a 15-yard scamper early in the fourth. Sanders hit 2,000 yards on a 2-yard run with 2:10 to play, and he left the game one play later, after a 53-yard jaunt to the Jets' 3-yard line, with 2,053 yards—the second most in NFL history at the time.

While Sanders's offensive line wore T-shirts that read "Mission Accomplished, 12-21-97, NFC playoffs, 2,000 yards," in the locker room after the game, the celebration was muted after Lions linebacker Reggie Brown suffered a career-ending neck injury early in the fourth quarter. Brown smashed headfirst into Jets guard Lamont Burns and lay motionless on the ground for several minutes.

Lions receiver Johnnie Morton ran to the tunnel looking for an ambulance, and ran back on the field with a stretcher. "I was panicking because we saw he wasn't breathing," Morton said. Dr. Terry Lock gave Brown mouth-to-mouth after he saw Brown's lips turning blue. And Brown underwent surgery to fuse vertebrae in his neck days later.

Barry Sanders is carried off the field by teammates after he became the third player in NFL history to rush for over 2,000 yards in a season.
COURTESY OF GETTY IMAGES

A week after the game, Sanders became the first Lions player to win Associated Press MVP. He shared the award with Brett Favre, with each getting 18 votes from a panel of 48 sportswriters and broadcasters. One Detroit voter who cast his ballot for Favre explained that votes were due the Tuesday before the regular season finale and he would have voted for Sanders had he been able to wait till after Sanders reached the 2,000-yard milestone.

DECEMBER 28, 1997

ANOTHER INJURY SCARE, ANOTHER PLAYOFF LOSS

THE LIONS suffered another injury scare a week later in their 20–10 playoff loss to the Buccaneers, when Scott Mitchell was carted off the field with his neck immobilized on the final play of the third quarter.

Mitchell was injured as he was trying to scramble for a first down and his head hit the leg of Bucs defensive tackle Brad Culpepper. He stayed on the ground for about 20 minutes and was taken to a local hospital, where he was treated for a mild brain injury and spent the night for evaluation.

"Everyone's thinking, 'Oh no, not two weeks in a row,'" receiver Johnnie Morton told the *Florida Sun-Sentinel*. "Even the Tampa Bay fans were thinking what was happening to our team."

Mitchell completed 10 of 25 passes for 78 yards before his injury, and the Bucs held Sanders to 65 yards rushing for the game as they raced to a 20–0 lead. Frank Reich replaced Mitchell and led a late touchdown drive, but the Lions still lost their fifth straight playoff game.

Defensive tackles Brad Culpepper (left) and Warren Sapp of the Tampa Bay Buccaneers put pressure on quarterback Scott Mitchell.
COURTESY OF GETTY IMAGES

NOVEMBER 8, 1998

"I DON'T COACH THAT STUFF"

OF ALL the meltdowns Lions coaches have had over the years, none was more epic than Bobby Ross's rant after a midseason loss to the Eagles in 1998.

The Lions gave up 219 yards rushing to the NFL's last-ranked offense and had one first down in a listless first half. As sloppy as they were, the Lions still had a chance to win at the end but committed four penalties on their final drive: two holding calls on tight end David Sloan, an illegal forward pass by Charlie Batch, and a false start on offensive tackle Tony Ramirez.

Jason Hanson missed the potential game-winning 58-yard field goal short, and the Lions went back to Detroit with a 2–7 record following a 10–9 defeat.

"That was terrible what we did out there today!" Ross said after the game, via the *Free Press*. "We shot ourselves in that last drive! We get two holding penalties, a motion penalty—you think I coach that stuff? I don't coach that stuff! I work on that stuff! I spend time on that stuff! And I'm getting all the damn heat."

The heat barely subsided the rest of the season, and many saw Ross's meltdown as the beginning of the end of his time in Detroit.

Bobby Ross went 27–30 in parts of four seasons as Lions coach and had an epic meltdown after a 1998 loss to the Eagles.
COURTESY OF GETTY IMAGES

NOVEMBER 26, 1998

TAILS NEVER FAILS

LIONS LUCK has mostly meant bad luck through the years, but the team had good fortune smile upon it for the overtime coin flip of a Thanksgiving game against the Steelers on November 26, 1998.

Steelers running back Jerome Bettis double-called the flip, first starting to say heads, then calling tails as the coin was in the air. Referee Phil Luckett administered the call as heads, and when the coin landed on tails gave the Lions the choice to kick or receive.

Bettis protested immediately, but the Lions took the ball, marched downfield, and seven plays later sent Jason Hanson out for the game-winning 42-yard field goal and a 19–16 victory.

Bettis called the coin flip "the most bizarre situation that I've ever been associated with," but in audio of the midfield exchange enhanced by Pittsburgh TV station KDKA, the Detroit native could be heard saying "heads" before tails. Luckett wrote in his referee report, per *Referee* magazine via NFL.com, that he was "disappointed with what transpired, but I did what I felt was right."

The NFL changed its coin-flip procedures after the game, bringing extra officials to midfield for the toss and requiring the visiting team to call heads or tails before the flip.

Lions defensive lineman Kerwin Waldroup celebrates a play in front of referee Phil Luckett in the team's 1998 Thanksgiving win over the Steelers.
COURTESY OF THE DETROIT LIONS

JULY 27, 1999

BARRY SANDERS RETIRES

***"THE REASON** I am retiring is simple: my desire to exit the game is greater than my desire to remain in it. I have searched my heart through and through and feel comfortable with this decision."*

Barry Sanders, the greatest running back in NFL history, announced his retirement in shocking fashion when he faxed a statement to his hometown newspaper, the *Wichita Eagle*, on July 27, 1999.

Sanders was 31 at the time, and his announcement came on the eve of training camp with him still at the top of his game. He was coming off his fifth straight 1,400-yard rushing season and was 1,457 yards shy of Walter Payton's all-time rushing record.

As stunning as the news was—Sanders flew to London to avoid a media crush after the announcement, which left him and the organization at odds for years—it didn't catch everyone off guard.

Safety Ron Rice said in a 2018 interview that Sanders told him in a cab ride to dinner the night before the 1997 season finale against the Ravens that he was planning to retire and alluded to Bobby Ross's dictatorial ways as one of the reasons why. Running back Ron Rivers, who replaced Sanders as the starter in 1999, said in 2018 that Sanders told him retirement was possible that offseason. In response, Rivers said he asked Sanders to wait till closer to camp to do it so the Lions wouldn't go out and sign a replacement. And Ross even had an idea it was coming, saying in 1999 he called Sanders 10 times and sent him three or four handwritten notes trying to ascertain his plans for the season with no response.

Sanders finished his NFL career with 15,269 yards rushing and 99 touchdowns. He ranks fourth on the NFL's all-time rushing list and is one of two players to play at least 10 seasons and make the Pro Bowl every year, according to ESPN. A six-time first-team All-Pro and two-time NFL Offensive Player of the Year, he was elected to the Hall of Fame in 2004.

Barry Sanders stunned the NFL when he retired on the eve of training camp in July of 1999.
COURTESY OF GETTY IMAGES

A mural of running back Barry Sanders in downtown Detroit. At the time of his retirement, Sanders needed 1,458 rushing yards to break Walter Payton's record and become the NFL's all-time leading rusher.
COURTESY OF GETTY IMAGES

JANUARY 8, 2000

A GLIMMER OF FALSE HOPE

BARRY SANDERS'S retirement left the Lions with a big hole at running back but also galvanized a team most everyone had left for dead entering the season.

The Lions won back-to-back games to start the year and were 6–2 at the halfway mark. They slumped down the stretch but still made the playoffs as a wild card with an 8–8 record, where they drew Washington again in the first round.

Like the 1991 NFC championship game, the rematch was a blowout almost from the opening kick. The Lions committed drive-extending running-into-the-kicker and pass-interference penalties on Washington's first possession and trailed 27–0 at halftime.

Stephen Davis ran for 119 yards and two touchdowns before leaving with a knee injury for Washington, and the Lions scored their only points in the fourth quarter on Ron Rice's 94-yard blocked field goal return and Gus Frerotte's 5-yard touchdown pass to Ron Rivers in a 27–13 loss.

Charlie Batch missed five games with a fractured thumb and the Lions slumped to 20th in the league in rushing without Sanders, but the playoff appearance gave the franchise a glimmer of what turned out to be false hope heading into the new millennium.

Washington running back Stephen Davis carries the ball during the first-round NFC playoff game against the Lions. COURTESY OF GETTY IMAGES

NOVEMBER 6, 2000

"WE HAVE THE WRONG COACH"

A LITTLE more than 15 months after Sanders walked away from the NFL, the Lions found themselves dealing with another surprise retirement.

On November 6, 2000, Bobby Ross told a shocked locker room his mind and body had tired to the point he could not coach anymore. The Lions were 5–4 at the time but were coming off demoralizing losses to the Colts and Dolphins. Asked after the Miami game why his team no-showed in a 23–8 defeat, Ross told reporters, "We have the wrong coach."

The 63-year-old Ross was dealing with health problems at the time of his retirement. He was treated for blood clots in his leg before the season and injured his back in training camp. He finished 27–30 as Lions coach, went 0–2 in the postseason, and never recaptured the magic he had in leading Georgia Tech to a college football championship and the Chargers to the Super Bowl.

Ford appointed Gary Moeller as Ross's replacement, giving him a three-year contract and carte blanche to make whatever personnel or staff changes he saw fit. The Lions won their first three games under Moeller and entered the season finale needing a win to make the playoffs.

Lions team owner William Clay Ford, followed by head coach Gary Moeller and executive vice president and chief operating officer Chuck Schmidt, enter a news conference on November 6, 2000 to announce Bobby Ross's retirement.
COURTESY OF GETTY IMAGES

DECEMBER 24, 2000

KICK-STARTING A REGIME CHANGE

THE LIONS FELL just short of the playoffs in 2000, a failure that sent the franchise spiraling to depths no one could have imagined when their season ended cruelly in a Christmas Eve loss to the Bears.

The Lions raced to a 10–0 lead only to come undone with a slew of self-inflicted mistakes. Herman Moore dropped a long touchdown pass when he lost the ball in the lights. Charlie Batch left the game with a rib injury, and his replacement, Stoney Case, had two costly fourth-quarter turnovers. Mike Compton committed a late, drive-stalling penalty.

R. W. McQuarters returned a Case interception 61 yards for a touchdown to give the Bears a 20–17 lead with 6:31 to play, then forced a Case fumble near midfield with less than a minute left and the game tied at 20. The Bears converted a fourth-and-1 on the ensuing drive, then sent rookie kicker Paul Edinger on for the game-winning 54-yard field goal with 2 seconds on the clock for a 23–20 victory.

Days after the game, William Clay Ford and his son, Bill Ford Jr., decided to roll the dice on an organizational overhaul that would set the franchise back for a decade.

Johnnie Morton (left), Larry Foster (center), and Tracy Scroggins sit dejected on the b ench after falling short of the playoffs with a 23–20 loss to the Chicago Bears.
COURTESY OF GETTY IMAGES

JANUARY 9, 2001

LIONS "ROLL THE DICE" ON MATT MILLEN

BILL FORD JR. called it "a roll of the dice," and for a franchise that had trafficked in the conventional for most of its 60-plus years of existence, it was a big one.

On January 9, 2001, the Lions hired Matt Millen as president and CEO, giving the Fox television and CBS radio analyst total control of football operations even though he had never been in an NFL front office before. The hire was the culmination of a two-year recruiting process started by Ford Jr. in 1999 but dismissed at that time when Bobby Ross threatened to retire.

With Ross out of the picture and the Lions stuck in mediocrity, William Clay Ford decided to reach out to Millen again after the Bears loss and moved quickly to hire the affable TV and radio personality.

General manager Matt Millen and owner William Clay Ford on the sidelines during the 2005 Thanksgiving Day game.
COURTESY OF GETTY IMAGES

Millen had been a highly successful player, winning four Super Bowls in his 12-year career, and was widely considered the heir apparent to John Madden on television. The Lions weren't the only team interested in bringing him into their organization. Washington and San Francisco also considered him for jobs.

"We've been nibbling at (success), but we haven't taken that extra step, and I believe the addition of Matt will provide the incentive we need and the knowledge we need to make that next step," Ford Jr. told the *Free Press* at the time of the hire.

Millen inherited a 9–7 team that just missed the playoffs and spent the next seven-plus seasons running it into the ground. He fired Gary Moeller as coach in one of his first acts as president, hired 49ers offensive coordinator Marty Mornhinweg as his replacement, and watched the team plummet to a 2–14 record, their first of 10 straight losing seasons, in his first year in charge.

The Lions went 31–81 under Millen before he was fired three weeks into the 2008 season, and Millen later admitted he was unqualified for and never should have taken the job.

APRIL 20, 2002

"BLUE SKIES" AHEAD

THE LIONS' decades-long search for a franchise quarterback took another turn in 2002 when they selected Joey Harrington with the third pick of the draft.

Harrington was not considered a can't-miss prospect; he had completed less than 55% of his passes as a starter at Oregon. And there was plenty of internal debate in Detroit between Harrington and Texas cornerback Quentin Jammer.

Bill Ford Jr. denied influencing the pick, though news reports in the days leading up to the draft suggested the Lions were comfortable proceeding with Mike McMahon under center. Marty Mornhinweg was a staunch supporter of the pick, telling ESPN that Harrington had "special tools, mentally and physically."

"He can make all the throws, everyone knows that, but what he has goes beyond throwing the football," Mornhinweg said. "Joey has great poise and leadership. Even on tape, you can see his team rallying up around him."

Harrington's poise and leadership did not translate to the NFL. He went 18–37 in four seasons as starter with the Lions, led the league with 22 interceptions in 2003, and was derisively nicknamed Joey Blue Skies by fans and media because of his unwavering positivity even as things burned around him.

Lions quarterback Joey Harrington entering the field during player introductions.
COURTESY OF GETTY IMAGES

AUGUST 24, 2002

NEW DIGS IN DETROIT

BY THE mid-1990s, playing in the Silverdome had become a financial drain on the Lions. Unlike most teams, the Lions derived no income from luxury suites, parking, or concessions, and in December of 1995 team management told then–Detroit mayor Dennis Archer it wanted to begin discussions about relocating to the city.

On August 20, 1996, the Lions announced plans to build what would be the 38th domed stadium in the world (and sixth in the NFL) on land adjacent to where a new open-air baseball stadium was planned for the Tigers.

Initially projected to cost $245 million, construction on the $500 million stadium launched November 16, 1999, and Ford Field opened less than three years later with modern dining and merchandise options, a glass atrium that offered views of the city's skyline, and luxury suites tucked into the brick wall of the old Hudson's warehouse that was incorporated into the stadium's design.

The Lions played their first preseason game at Ford Field on August 24, 2002, against the Steelers, and held their first regular-season game there September 22 against the Packers. Az-Zahir Hakim scored the game's first touchdown on a punt return, but Joey Harrington threw four interceptions as Green Bay scored 17 straight points to open the second half for a 37–31 victory.

In the more than 20 years since its opening, Ford Field has hosted the Super Bowl, the Final Four, the Frozen Four, and WrestleMania, and it has become one of the region's major concert and entertainment venues.

Ford Field and Comerica Park.
COURTESY OF GETTY IMAGES

NOVEMBER 24, 2002

GONE WITH THE WIND

MARTY MORNHINWEG lasted just two seasons and won only five games in Detroit. The low point of his tenure came in a 20–17 loss to the Bears on November 24, 2002, at the University of Illinois, when the Lions won the overtime coin flip and opted to take the wind.

"I had great confidence in our defense to get a stop and [force the Bears to] punt into the wind," he explained to the *Free Press*. "Allow our field goal kicker to have the wind."

The game never got that far as the Bears returned the opening kick to their own 35-yard line, crossed midfield two plays later, and sent Paul Edinger on for the game-winning 40-yard field goal without the Lions ever touching the ball.

Mornhinweg's strategy might have worked, if not for his own greed. The Lions forced an incomplete pass on third-and-8 from their 35-yard line, but Morhinweg accepted a 10-yard holding penalty on the play. Bears quarterback Jim Miller completed a 15-yard pass to Marty Booker one snap later, then converted a fourth-and-3 to keep the drive alive.

Edinger said after the game his max distance on field goal tries into the 17-mph wind was 43 yards, and Mornhinweg admitted he was wrong to play for field position on the accepted penalty.

Lions head coach Marty Mornhinweg looks on from the sidelines.
COURTESY OF GETTY IMAGES

FEBRUARY 4, 2003

LIONS LAND STEVE MARIUCCI

AS UGLY as the Lions' 5-27 record was under Marty Mornhinweg, Matt Millen initially opted to keep his head coach for a third season—only to abruptly change course when the 49ers fired Steve Mariucci after a second-round playoff loss to the Buccaneers.

The Lions fired Mornhinweg on January 27, 2003, days after he and his staff coached in the Senior Bowl college all-star game, and hired Mariucci—an Iron Mountain, Michigan, native who went 57-39 in six seasons as 49ers coach—eight days later.

While the hire was roundly considered an upgrade, the Lions drew the ire of civil rights attorneys Cyrus Mehri and Johnnie Cochran for running afoul of the NFL's Rooney Rule with the deal. The Lions did not interview any minority candidates for the job, with several refusing to take part in what they believed were sham interviews.

The NFL fined Millen $200,000 for ignoring its new diversity guidelines, which required teams to interview at least one minority candidate for head coaching positions.

Though popular with some veterans for his laid-back approach, Mariucci fared little better than Mornhinweg on the field, going 15-28 as Lions coach before he was fired 11 games into the 2005 season.

Lions head coach Steve Mariucci smiles while meeting with the media on February 5, 2003 at Ford Field.
COURTESY OF GETTY IMAGES

MILLEN'S LOVE AFFAIR WITH FIRST-ROUND RECEIVERS

MATT MILLEN NEVER quite grasped the concept of building a well-rounded roster. Case in point: his decision to spend three straight first-round picks on receivers Charles Rogers (No. 2 overall), Roy Williams (No. 7), and Mike Williams (No. 10) in the 2003–05 drafts.

The Rogers pick was understandable. He was the best non-quarterback prospect in the 2003 draft after a star-studded career at Michigan State, and Harrington needed a young receiver to grow with. Rogers caught two touchdowns in his NFL debut, but broke his collarbone in practice his rookie season and played just 10 games the rest of his career. He reinjured his collarbone in Week 1 of the 2004 season, was suspended for violating the league's drug policy in 2005, and succumbed to a slew of problems off the field.

The Roy Williams pick was bold. Williams was well-regarded coming out of Texas, and the Lions envisioned being an offensive power. He played 4½ productive seasons in Detroit and made one Pro Bowl (when he had 82 catches and 1,310 yards in 2006) before he was traded to the Cowboys in 2008 for three draft picks, including a first-rounder.

The Mike Williams pick was a head-scratcher. Williams followed in Maurice Clarett's footsteps and declared for the NFL draft as a sophomore, but was denied entry and forced to sit out the 2004 college season after an appeals court upheld the NFL policy requiring early entrants to be three years removed from high school. He was a Rogers-like bust, battling weight issues and work-ethic problems while catching 35 passes for 449 yards in two seasons with the Lions. Worst of all, the Lions passed on Hall of Fame pass rusher DeMarcus Ware to draft him.

Charles Rogers, the first of three straight wide receivers Matt Millen drafted in the first round from 2003-05, talks with reporters after a game.
COURTESY OF GETTY IMAGES

DECEMBER 18, 2005

UNMOVED BY THE MILLEN MAN MARCH

MATT MILLEN was entering the final year of the five-year contract he got to leave the TV booth, with an unsightly record of 16–48, when William Clay Ford gave him a five-year extension on August 4, 2005.

"We want continuity in here," Ford told the *Free Press*. "I think Matt has built a great foundation for us to move forward, and I can't think of anybody better to see it through than Matt."

The extension infuriated Lions fans, even those who had lived through Ford's perplexing loyalty to Russ Thomas and Wayne Fontes. And when another Lions season began circling the drain late in the 2005 season, local radio station WDFN 1130-AM organized a protest they dubbed the Millen Man March.

Before the Lions' home finale against the Bengals, hundreds of fans gathered at a nearby bar and made the five-block walk to the stadium carrying signs and wearing shirts that read "Fire Millen." The crowd swelled to more than 1,000 by the time they reached Ford Field with chants of, "Ho, ho, ho, Millen must go," and inside much of the stadium wore orange hunter's gear, the Bengals' color.

The Lions finished the season with six losses in their final seven games, Steve Mariucci was fired in late November, and Dick Jauron took over as interim coach. Ownership, however, was unmoved by the march and on January 19, 2006, Millen picked Rod Marinelli as the team's next head coach.

A young fan holds up a sign to fire Matt Millen, president and CEO of the Lions.
COURTESY OF GETTY IMAGES

APRIL 28, 2007

FOURTH TIME'S A CHARM

THE LIONS had the No. 2 pick of the 2007 draft after going 3–13 in Rod Marinelli's first season, and for the fourth time in five years, they used their top-10 choice on a wide receiver.

"The last few years, it may not have worked out," Calvin Johnson said on draft night of the Lions' penchant for spending high picks on pass catchers, via the *Free Press*. "But I'm sure my situation will."

Johnson was no ordinary receiver. He was 6 feet 5, 239 pounds, ran a 4.35-second 40-yard dash, and was so freakishly gifted Roy Williams nicknamed him "Megatron" as a rookie.

Then–Lions offensive coordinator Mike Martz called Johnson "the best [receiver prospect] I've ever seen," and after a modest start to his career with 48 catches for 756 yards in 2007, Johnson quickly made his case as one of the best receivers ever.

Blessed with a relentless work ethic and Barry Sanders–like humility, Johnson tied for the NFL lead with 12 receiving touchdowns in his second season and posted the first of seven 1,000-yard receiving seasons in his nine-year career. He made the Pro Bowl in each of his final six seasons, was a three-time first-team All-Pro selection, and in 2021 joined Randy Moss, Jerry Rice, Steve Largent, Paul Warfield, Lance Alworth, and Raymond Berry as the only first-ballot receivers in the Hall of Fame.

Calvin Johnson holds up a No. 1 jersey after being selected by the Lions with the second pick in the 2007 NFL draft.
COURTESY OF GETTY IMAGES

OCTOBER 12, 2008

DAN ORLOVSKY AND THE SELF SAFETY

DAN ORLOVSKY'S first career NFL start was a memorable one.

A fifth-round pick out of UConn in 2005, Orlovsky spent three seasons toiling on the bench before he was thrust into the starting lineup for an injured Jon Kitna on October 12, 2008, against the Vikings. He threw his first career touchdown pass that day to Calvin Johnson, who gave him the ball to spike in celebration. He took six sacks behind a sieve of an offensive line. And he ran out of the back of his own end zone for a safety.

Late in the first quarter of a scoreless game, with the Lions facing third-and-10 from their own 1-yard line, Orlovsky took a shotgun snap from center Dominic Raiola and rolled to his right to avoid pressure from 2007 NFL sack leader Jared Allen.

Orlovsky lost track of his spot on the field as he ran out of bounds across the back line with Allen pointing his direction in celebration.

"When they started blowing the whistle, I was like, 'Did we false start or were they offsides or something?'" Orlovsky told the *Free Press* after the game, a 12–10 loss. "And I looked, and I was just like, 'You're an idiot.'"

Now an ESPN analyst, Orlovsky has been a good sport about his gaffe in retirement. He kept a picture of Allen on his bookshelf for remote shots during the COVID pandemic and writes "endzones should be 11 yards" in his bio on social media.

Jared Allen of the Vikings chases Dan Orlovsky out of bounds for a safety during a game in Minnesota.
COURTESY OF GETTY IMAGES

2008

THE WORST TEAM IN NFL HISTORY

THE 75TH SEASON in Detroit Lions history was also the franchise's worst.

The Lions went into the season with renewed optimism coming off a 7–9 year. They went undefeated in the preseason, then became the first team in NFL history to go 0–16.

Matt Millen was fired three games into the season. Martin Mayhew and Tom Lewand were promoted to general manager and team president, respectively. Roy Williams was traded. Jon Kitna went on injured reserve. Three different quarterbacks started games. And the defense allowed 517 points, the second-most in NFL history at the time.

A dejected Lions bench near end of an 0–16 season.
COURTESY OF GETTY IMAGES

The Lions lost 10 games by double digits in 2008 and did not score a first-quarter point until the seventh game of the season. The Vikings game was their only loss by a field goal or less, and the Lions went to Lambeau Field in Week 17 needing a win over the Packers to avoid becoming the second team to go winless in a non-strike season in the Super Bowl era.

On a frigid 22-degree day, the Packers jumped to a 14–0 lead and scored 17 fourth-quarter points to pull away with a 31–21 victory. The Lions became the first team in NFL history to allow two 100-yard rushers and two 100-yard receivers in the same game, and Jason Hanson told MLive.com the entire organization was "embarrassed" by the outcome.

"I think the record speaks for itself," Rod Marinelli said after the game, per the *New York Times*. "We have nobody to point a finger at other than ourselves."

Marinelli was fired a day later with a 10–38 record, and Mayhew and Lewand were given full-time roles and put in charge of the Lions' rebuild.

APRIL 25, 2009

LIONS TAKE MATTHEW STAFFORD NO. 1 OVERALL

FIFTY-ONE YEARS after Bobby Layne may or may not have cursed the franchise, and a few months after they bottomed out with the worst season in NFL history, cosmic forces seemed to be at play with the Lions' No. 1 pick in the 2009 draft.

The prize that year was Georgia quarterback Matthew Stafford, a rocket-armed gunslinger who starred at the same Highland Park High that Layne attended and led the school to its first state championship since 1957.

Stafford wasn't a slam dunk No. 1 pick. The Lions also considered Wake Forest linebacker Aaron Curry and Baylor offensive tackle Jason Smith, and fans booed the choice at the team's Ford Field draft party.

But new Lions coach Jim Schwartz said before he was hired that it was "time to find a replacement for Bobby Layne," and Stafford fit the bill.

The Lions finalized a six-year, $78 million contract with Stafford the night before the draft and made him their starting quarterback in Week 1 of the 2009 season. Stafford played 12 seasons in Detroit, made one Pro Bowl—one of just three Lions quarterbacks since Layne selected for the game—led the team to three playoff appearances, and ranks as the franchise leader in every major statistical passing category.

Matthew Stafford pitches the ball to Kevin Smith against the Chicago Bears.
COURTESY OF GETTY IMAGES

NOVEMBER 22, 2009

A SHOULDER TO LEAN ON

IT DIDN'T take long for Matthew Stafford to endear himself to Lions fans.

He led the Lions to a 19–14 win over Washington in his third career start that snapped the team's 19-game losing streak, and two months later he engineered a dramatic 38–37 come-from-behind win over the Browns in a moment immortalized by NFL Films.

The Lions fell behind 24–3 in the first quarter and trailed 37–31 when Stafford returned from a sprained left non-throwing shoulder to throw the game-winning touchdown with no time on the clock.

Stafford injured his shoulder on a Hail Mary attempt one play before the TD. He rolled to his left and spun out of one tackle, then back to his right and sidestepped another before launching a pass downfield. Defensive tackle C.J. Mosley hit Stafford as he threw, driving Stafford's shoulder into the ground, but officials flagged cornerback Hank Poteat for pass interference in the end zone to give the Lions an untimed down from the 1-yard line.

When the Browns took a timeout as trainers tended to Stafford on the sideline, Stafford sprung to his feet and ran past doctors back onto the field where he threw the game-winning touchdown to Brandon Pettigrew.

Stafford finished with a Lions rookie record 422 yards and five touchdowns, and he earned the respect of everyone in the locker room.

"It shows how much heart he has," Pettigrew told the *Free Press* after the game. "He's the guy."

Matthew Stafford gets up after being injured against the Cleveland Browns.
COURTESY OF GETTY IMAGES

2010

A BOY NAMED SUH

WHILE MATTHEW Stafford's star was flickering through two injury-riddled seasons, the Lions found a new cornerstone for their defense in Ndamukong Suh, the second pick of the 2010 draft.

A Heisman Trophy finalist in his final season at Nebraska, Suh was a menacing force on the Lions defensive line from the moment he stepped on the field as a rookie. He had a team-high 10 sacks in 2010, the most of any interior lineman in the NFL; he was runaway winner of Defensive Rookie of the Year; and his name became a war cry—"Suuuuuuuh"—for fans in Detroit.

Suh gave the Lions defense a much-needed attitude, even if his play sometimes bordered on dirty. He was fined in the preseason for flinging Browns quarterback Jake Delhomme to the ground by the facemask and again in the regular season when he hit Jay Cutler in the back of the neck with a violent two-hand shove.

Suh had 36 sacks in five seasons with Detroit and earned three first-team All-Pro honors. He also attempted an extra point as a rookie after Jason Hanson suffered a knee injury in an overtime loss to the Jets—the kick missed off the upright—and returned a fumble 17 yards for a touchdown in a 2010 win over Washington.

Defensive lineman Ndamukong Suh looks on from the sideline during a preseason game.
COURTESY OF GETTY IMAGES

SEPTEMBER 12, 2010

CALVIN JOHNSON AND THE CATCH

MATTHEW STAFFORD missed six games his rookie season with knee and shoulder injuries, and most of the 2010 season after he injured his throwing shoulder in the Lions' season-opening loss to the Bears. He was hurt on a blindside hit by Julius Peppers with 20 seconds left in the first half and watched the final two quarters from the sideline with his right arm in a sling.

The Bears took a 19–14 lead on Jay Cutler's 28-yard touchdown pass to Matt Forte with 1:32 to play, setting the stage for one of the most controversial finishes in NFL history.

Calvin Johnson appeared to score the go-ahead touchdown for the Lions with 24 seconds left when he outjumped Zackary Bowman for a Shaun Hill pass in the corner of the end zone. Johnson high-pointed the ball, landed with both feet on the ground, then fell backward on his left hip with the ball securely in his right hand.

The ball squirted loose when Johnson brought his right hand to the ground as he sprang to his feet and sprinted across the back of the end zone in celebration, unaware that officials had convened to rule the play an incomplete pass because he did not complete the "process" of the catch.

"I figured that if I got two feet and a knee down, to me it's a catch," Johnson said after the game. "That's why I got up and took off."

While the play was ruled correctly according to NFL rules at the time, it looked enough like a catch that it sparked a years-long controversy about what was and wasn't a complete pass.

When the NFL redefined a catch in 2018 to have three parts—control of the ball, two feet or another body part down, and making or having the ability to make a football move—Johnson applauded what's commonly known as the Calvin Johnson Rule, saying it "took them seven years to figure out what we knew on Day 1."

Calvin Johnson has the ball securely in his right hand as he tumbles to the ground on what was ruled an incomplete pass in a 2010 game against the Bears.

COURTESY OF GETTY IMAGES

OCTOBER 10, 2011

BACK IN PRIME TIME WITH A BANG

THE LIONS were so bad for most of the 2000s they were persona non grata when it came to prime-time games. But they showed enough life late in the 2010 season, winning their final four games without Matthew Stafford, to get back in the Monday-night rotation early in the 2011 season.

On October 10, 2011, the Lions hosted the Bears in their first Monday Night Football game in more than a decade. They brought ring announcer Michael Buffer in to do pregame introductions, they named Barry Sanders honorary captain, and the Ford Field crowd was so earsplitting it caused nine false-start penalties on the Bears.

Calvin Johnson opened the scoring with a 73-yard touchdown catch from Stafford, and running back Jahvid Best had an 88-yard touchdown run and two more long gains—runs of 43 and 15 yards—to put the game away in the fourth quarter.

The Lions cruised to a 24–13 victory, their fifth straight to open the season, and seemed well on their way to their first playoff appearance in 12 years.

Jahvid Best celebrates his third-quarter touchdown with Nate Burleson while playing the Chicago Bears.
COURTESY OF GETTY IMAGES

OCTOBER 16, 2011

SCHWARTZ, HARBAUGH, AND THE HANDSHAKE

THE LIONS' winning streak came to an end in Week 6 with a 25–19 loss to the 49ers.

San Francisco scored the go-ahead touchdown on a 6-yard pass from Alex Smith to Delanie Walker with 1:51 to play, added an insurance field goal 49 seconds later after turning the Lions over on downs, then stopped Detroit again as time expired on a botched lateral 70 yards from the end zone.

49ers coach Jim Harbaugh ran on the field in celebration and slapped Lions coach Jim Schwartz on the back as the two exchanged postgame handshakes. Schwartz took offense to the backslap and chased Harbaugh about 25 yards downfield into the back of the end zone, bumping him along the way, before players from both teams separated the coaches before reaching the tunnel.

"Obviously you win a game like that you're excited and things like that, but I think there's a protocol that goes with this league," Schwartz said.

Harbaugh, who grew up in Michigan and briefly played for the Lions in 2001, said after the game he was at fault for the exchange.

"Is there two more passionate coaches in the NFL?" Lions receiver Nate Burleson said. "Both of those guys are high energy and love to show emotion on game day. So it didn't surprise me."

Jim Harbaugh, head coach of the San Francisco 49ers, argues with Jim Schwartz of the Lions during a game at Ford Field on October 16, 2011.
COURTESY OF GETTY IMAGES

NOVEMBER 24, 2011

THE STOMP SEEN ROUND THE WORLD

ONE OF Ndamukong Suh's signature moments as a Lion came on November 24, 2011, in his second Thanksgiving game.

After Aaron Rodgers threw incomplete on third-and-goal from the 3-yard line on the Packers' opening drive of the second half, Suh became entangled with Packers guard Evan Dietrich-Smith. The two wrestled to the ground, then Suh pushed Dietrich-Smith's helmet into the turf three times as he stood up and stomped on Dietrich-Smith's arm before walking away.

Suh was ejected, fined, and suspended two games, and he defiantly defended his actions in an ill-advised postgame news conference, saying he would only apologize to his teammates, coaches, and "true fans" while insisting he did no wrong.

"What I did was remove myself from the situation the best way I felt, with me being held down in the situation that I was in," Suh said. "My intentions were not to kick anybody as I did not. . . . As you see, I'm walking away from the situation."

With Suh out of the game, the Lions fell apart. Green Bay scored two plays later to take a 14–0 lead, and Matthew Stafford threw interceptions on the Lions' next two possessions as the Packers ran away with a 27–15 victory.

Ndamukong Suh looks on while Lions head coach Jim Schwartz and NFL referee Terry McAulay talk over Suh's ejection from the game against the Green Bay Packers at Ford Field.
COURTESY OF GETTY IMAGES

2011

STAFFORD JOINS EXCLUSIVE COMPANY

Matthew Stafford passes against the San Francisco 49ers.
COURTESY OF GETTY IMAGES

MATTHEW STAFFORD underwent shoulder surgery and missed 13 games in 2010, but he returned in 2011 to have the best statistical season of his career.

Voted the NFL's Comeback Player of the Year, Stafford set franchise records with 5,038 yards passing and 41 touchdowns, and he joined Drew Brees, Tom Brady, and Dan Marino as the fourth player in NFL history to eclipse 5,000 yards in a season.

He led the league with 663 pass attempts—both Brees and Brady had more yards that season—and silenced questions about his health by playing all 16 games for the first time in his career, the start of an ironman streak that would run 136 games and last until the 2019 season.

As gaudy as his numbers were, Stafford seemed like a long shot to reach 5,000 yards late in the year. He entered a Week 16 game against the San Diego Chargers with 4,145 yards passing, then threw for 373 yards and three touchdowns in a playoff-clinching win. One week later, Stafford had a career-high 520 yards passing—the sixth-highest single-game total in NFL history at the time—and five touchdowns in a loss to the Packers that cemented his spot in the record books.

JANUARY 1, 2012

THE MATT FLYNN GAME

MATTHEW STAFFORD'S record-setting performance came in an otherwise deflating game for the Lions.

Playing at Lambeau Field against a Packers team resting key starters Aaron Rodgers, Charles Woodson, Clay Matthews, and Greg Jennings, the Lions had a chance to clinch the fifth seed in the NFL playoffs but couldn't stop backup Packers quarterback Matt Flynn, who set franchise records with 480 yards passing and six touchdowns in a 45–41 Green Bay victory.

The game was an unexpected shootout in below-freezing temperatures and 20-mph winds. Stafford completed 36 of 59 passes, Calvin Johnson had 11 catches for 244 yards, and Titus Young caught two touchdowns for the Lions, who used both their challenges in the first half and had no recourse when officials waved off a third Young TD, incorrectly ruling he did not have two feet inbounds.

The Lions fell to the six seed in the NFC and drew a wild-card matchup with the 13-win Saints. Had they won, they would have gone on the road to face the 9–7 Giants in the first round.

Flynn, who completed 31 of 44 passes in his second career start, parlayed his big day into a three-year, $20.5 million free agent deal with the Seattle Seahawks.

Matthew Stafford sets up to throw against the Green Bay Packers at Lambeau Field.
COURTESY OF GETTY IMAGES

JANUARY 7, 2012

AND THE SAINTS GO MARCHING ON

THE GIANTS went on a magical playoff run as the four seed and won Super Bowl XLVI, so maybe losing to Matt Flynn didn't matter. But the Lions' overmatched defense couldn't have drawn a worse opponent in their first playoff game since 1999 than the high-powered Saints.

Drew Brees had set an NFL record with 5,476 yards passing that season, and New Orleans had steamrolled the Lions in the regular season, 31–17.

The Lions kept things close for a half in the playoff rematch before their defense buckled again. Brees threw for 466 yards and three touchdowns, and the Saints scored on seven of their 10 possessions in a 45–28 rout. Calvin Johnson had a dominant playoff debut with 12 catches for 211 yards and two touchdowns, but the Lions allowed 626 yards of offense and did not force a punt. Along with their seven scores, the Saints fumbled twice and took a knee to end the game.

"It was a successful season, I think," Dominic Raiola said after the game. "I don't think anybody predicted us to go to the playoffs this year, but you never want to hang your hat on that. We said we weren't just happy to just be in the playoffs so we're disappointed right now."

Lions receiver Calvin Johnson making a catch against the Saints.
COURTESY OF GETTY IMAGES

NOVEMBER 22, 2012

ANOTHER CHALLENGING THANKSGIVING DEFEAT

NDAMUKONG SUH committed another foot foul in the Lions' 2012 Thanksgiving loss to the Houston Texans when he kicked quarterback Matt Schaub in the groin. He insisted the kick was inadvertent and was fined but not suspended for the play.

The game is more remembered, though, for the flub Jim Schwartz made on Justin Forsett's 81-yard touchdown run that shouldn't have been in the third quarter. Forsett appeared to be stopped by two Lions defenders after a short gain, but popped to his feet when officials did not blow the play dead and outran Lawrence Jackson to the end zone.

Schwartz angrily threw a challenge flag on the play, which by rule negated the automatic review due on all scoring plays. Replays clearly showed Forsett was down, but the touchdown stood and the Lions were penalized 15 yards for unsportsmanlike conduct.

"That's all my fault," Schwartz said after the game. "I overreacted in that situation and I cost us a touchdown."

Schwartz compounded that mistake in overtime when he sent Jason Hanson out for a 47-yard field goal on third-and-11 with just over 4 minutes to play. Hanson's kick hit the right upright, and the Texans took possession at their own 37 and made the game-winning 32-yard field goal six plays later.

Lions head coach Jim Schwartz talks with official Jerry Bergman during a disputed play during the game against the Houston Texans at Ford Field on November 22, 2012.
COURTESY OF GETTY IMAGES

DECEMBER 22, 2012

CALVIN JOHNSON SOARS PAST JERRY RICE

BARRY SANDERS had 2,000 yards rushing; Calvin Johnson almost had 2,000 yards receiving.

Johnson broke Jerry Rice's single-season receiving record in 2012 when he became the first receiver in NFL history to top 1,900 yards. Johnson finished the season with 122 catches for 1,964 yards, tied or set NFL marks for most 100-yard games in a season (11) and most consecutive 100-yard games (eight), and did it while dispelling the "Madden curse" after appearing on the cover of the popular video game that year.

Johnson had two 200-yard games in the final eight weeks of the season, and he broke Rice's record with a memorable 11-catch, 225-yard performance in a Week 16 loss to the Falcons. After breaking the record on a 26-yard catch and run late in the fourth quarter, Johnson jogged to the Lions sideline and handed the ball to his father, Calvin Johnson Sr., before heading back to the huddle.

"I've been an NFL fan my entire life," Jim Schwartz said after the game. "I grew up in Baltimore with Hall of Famers like Johnny Unitas and Raymond Berry and a lot of other guys; great players in the history of the National Football League. I've coached for 19 years in the NFL. I've never seen a better player than Calvin Johnson."

Johnson finished the season with a five-catch, 72-yard game against the Bears, and the Lions missed the playoffs with a 4–12 record.

Wide receiver Calvin Johnson with with his father, Calvin Johnson Sr., after breaking Jerry Rice's single-season receiving record against the Atlanta Falcons.
COURTESY OF GETTY IMAGES

OCTOBER 27, 2013

THE FAKE SPIKE AND ANOTHER MEGATRON MILESTONE

CALVIN JOHNSON had the best single-game performance of his career on October 27, 2013, when he caught 14 passes for a whopping 329 yards in a 31–30 win over the Cowboys. It was the second-most yards by a receiver in a game in NFL history, and the most by any player in regulation. Flipper Anderson had 336 yards in a 1989 game, but 40 of those came in overtime.

Johnson opened the scoring with a 2-yard touchdown on fourth-and-goal and made one of his patented jump-ball catches over two Cowboys defenders, but his biggest grab was a 22-yard reception with 30 seconds left that set up the Lions' dramatic game-winning touchdown.

Out of timeouts and with the clock ticking, Matthew Stafford frantically tried to get his teammates to the line of scrimmage to spike the ball and kill the clock after Johnson's catch. Left tackle Riley Reiff, who thought Johnson scored and was celebrating downfield, was last to arrive, and when Stafford took the snap from Dominic Raiola with 14 seconds left, he leaped over his center's back and reached the ball across the goal line past an unsuspecting Cowboys defense for a touchdown.

"I told everybody I was spiking it," Stafford said. "I was screaming, 'Clock.' I was going to spike it. It was a feel thing. I was making a play, man. I was trying to help my team win and sure am glad I got across."

Quarterback Matthew Stafford breaks the plane of the goal to score a touchdown against the Dallas Cowboys.
COURTESY OF GETTY IMAGES

In his first year as head coach Jim Caldwell oversaw an immediate improvement in the Lions' defense.
COURTESY OF GETTY IMAGES

JANUARY 14, 2014

A NEW REGIME, A NEW-LOOK DEFENSE

THE LIONS lost six of their last seven games in 2013 and missed the playoffs for the second straight year. Jim Schwartz was fired the day after the season, and the Lions hired Jim Caldwell as his replacement.

Widely regarded as the team's No. 2 choice after Ken Whisenhunt spurned the Lions to coach the Tennessee Titans, Caldwell was the anti-Schwartz in many ways: an even-tempered, experienced former head coach who had cut his teeth as an offensive assistant, where he worked closely with Peyton Manning.

In Caldwell's first season in Detroit, the Lions transformed from an offensive juggernaut to one of the league's best defenses. They held opponents to a league-low 69.3 rushing yards per game in 2014, the third-lowest total since the NFL expanded to 32 teams in 2002. They finished third in the league in scoring defense (17.6 ppg) and tied for third with 20 interceptions.

Ndamukong Suh, playing out the final year of his rookie contract, was a first-team All-Pro selection; linebacker DeAndre Levy and safety Glover Quin earned second-team honors; and the Lions went 11–5 in the regular season, tied at the time for the second-most wins in franchise history.

DECEMBER 28, 2014

ANOTHER LAMBEAU LETDOWN, ANOTHER SUH SUSPENSION

THE LIONS were 11–4 and tied with the Packers atop the NFC North heading into another regular season finale at Green Bay's Lambeau Field. The winner would win the division and get a home playoff game, while the loser would be the six seed and travel to Dallas in the wild-card round.

The Packers scored the game's first 14 points, but Aaron Rodgers, on his way to his second MVP, aggravated a calf injury late in the first half to give the Lions life. Matthew Stafford threw touchdown passes to Calvin Johnson on the Lions' final drive of the second quarter and again to start the third, but Eddie Lacy ran for 100 yards on the Lions' league-best rush defense and Rodgers rallied Green Bay to 16 straight points for a 30–20 Packers victory.

Late in the game, Ndamukong Suh found himself embroiled in another controversy when he stepped on Rodgers's injured left calf twice. Suh knocked Rodgers to the ground on the play, then stepped backwards onto Rodgers's leg, first with his left heel and then with his right foot.

Though Suh was not penalized on the play, the NFL suspended him for one game. The suspension was overturned by an independent arbitrator, who did not buy Suh's claim it was an accident and fined him $70,000 but allowed him to play in the Lions' playoff game.

Ndamukong Suh during the second quarter of a game at Lambeau Field on December 28, 2014.
COURTESY OF GETTY IMAGES

JANUARY 4, 2015

THE PASS INTERFERENCE PENALTY THAT WASN'T

LIONS SAFETY James Ihedigbo called it "ridiculous," and enraged Lions fans had even more choice words for referee Pete Morelli and his crew after they bungled a pass interference call with 8:20 to play in the Lions' playoff loss to the Cowboys.

The Lions raced to a 20–7 lead and were up a field goal and driving when Matthew Stafford threw a third-and-1 pass to Brandon Pettigrew down the Cowboys sideline. Linebacker Anthony Hitchens was face-guarding Pettigrew on the play and made contact with the tight end before the ball arrived.

Back judge Lee Dyer flagged Hitchens for pass interference and Morelli announced the penalty and walked it off, only to have head linesman Jerry Bergman overrule Dyer and pick up the flag.

Rather than try and convert on fourth-and-1 from the Dallas 46, the Lions attempted to draw the Cowboys offsides and then punted from just beyond midfield. Sam Martin shanked the punt 10 yards, and Tony Romo drove the Cowboys for the winning touchdown on the ensuing possession to send the Lions to a 24–20 defeat.

"I don't ever think it really comes down to one call, but calls are crucial during games like this and everything's so tight and everything's on the line, a team's playing so hard, to have something that's so questionable that occurs, that's concerning," Jim Caldwell said.

The penalty gaffe wasn't the only reason the Lions lost. Calvin Johnson was open streaking across the middle of the field on the Pettigrew play; Martin's punt didn't help; the Cowboys converted a fourth-and-6 on their go-ahead drive; and Stafford fumbled twice in the final 2:10 to clinch the Lions' eighth straight playoff loss.

But the NFL acknowledged later Hitchens should have been called for a defensive holding penalty on the game-altering play.

"We get those yards there, who knows, we maybe go score a touchdown, the thing's out of reach," Stafford said. "But there were a lot of plays along the way here and there that if we just execute a little better in all phases on a few, we come away with a win."

Cowboys linebacker Anthony Hitchens sits on the ground after defending Lions tight end Brandon Pettigrew on the play. A flag was thrown but later picked up and no pass interference was called on the play.
COURTESY OF GETTY IMAGES

The Cowboys' Anthony Hitchens defends tight end Brandon Pettigrew during an NFC wild-card game at AT&T Stadium.
COURTESY OF GETTY IMAGES

2015

SUH SETS SAIL FOR SOUTH BEACH

NDAMUKONG SUH got emotional after the Lions' playoff loss, briefly walking out of his postgame news conference as his eyes welled with tears and then returning to finish speaking with the media.

"I'm speechless," he said. "I think this defense put it all out there, this team put it all out there and I just, like I said, I didn't expect this outcome. It's sickening."

Months later, with the benefit of hindsight, some in the organization felt Suh's emotion was the product not just of the season-ending loss but of knowing he had played his last game as a Lion.

After five dominant but divisive seasons in Detroit, Suh signed a record-setting free-agent deal with the Dolphins that made him the highest-paid defensive player in the NFL at roughly $19 million per season.

The Lions were not able to franchise Suh after restructuring his contract, and Suh's representatives never made the team a firm offer during negotiations that spanned more than a year.

With Suh gone, the Lions traded for Haloti Ngata as a replacement, but their defense never recovered from losing its tone-setter. The Lions started 1–7 in 2015 and finished in the bottom half of the NFL in total, scoring, and passing defense.

Defensive tackle Ndamukong Suh's five years in Detroit ended with his departure for Miami in 2015.
COURTESY OF GETTY IMAGES

NOVEMBER 1, 2015

AN INTERNATIONAL EMBARRASSMENT

THE LIONS fired offensive coordinator Joe Lombardi seven games into the 2015 season and bottomed out days later when they lost to the Chiefs 45–10 in London. Matthew Stafford threw two interceptions and took six sacks in a performance so embarrassing it prompted massive change when the team returned to the states.

Martha Firestone Ford, who had taken control of the franchise when William Clay Ford died on March 9, 2014, fired Martin Mayhew and Tom Lewand during the Lions' bye week and brought in trusted family advisor Rod Wood as team president.

With two NFL newcomers in charge, the Lions entrusted their general manager search to league-backed consultant Ernie Accorsi. They hired Patriots executive Bob Quinn after a narrow search, and after missing the wild-card week window to interview some coaching candidates, Quinn yielded to ownership's wishes and retained Jim Caldwell as coach.

The Lions won six of their final eight games to finish the season 7–9, and Sheila Ford Hamp, the second of the Fords' four children, started an apprenticeship around that time that would lead her to take over from her mother as the team's controlling owner in 2020.

The Chiefs' Charcandrick West celebrates after scoring a touchdown against the Lions in a game at Wembley Stadium in London.
COURTESY OF GETTY IMAGES

DECEMBER 3, 2015

HAIL NO HE DIDN'T

IN THE LIONS' long, tormented history, few losses have been as soul-crushing as the one they suffered on December 3, 2015, against the Packers.

After clawing back onto the fringes of playoff contention with three straight wins following their unsightly start and jumping to a 20–0 lead in a game at Ford Field, the Lions lost on a misplayed Hail Mary from Aaron Rodgers to Richard Rodgers following a disputed penalty.

The Packers were 79 yards from the end zone with 6 seconds to play when they attempted a desperation multilateral. Devin Taylor was flagged for a facemask penalty on Aaron Rodgers after the second lateral, giving Green Bay an extra untimed down from the 39-yard line. Replays showed that Taylor's thumb grazed Rodgers' facemask, but he took the quarterback down by his shoulders.

Not thinking Rodgers could heave the ball to the end zone, Jim Caldwell had his defense play for "that pass back and forth kind of thing" on Green Bay's final snap. Rodgers bought time scrambling against a three-man rush and launched a 61-yard bomb high into the rafters that Richard Rodgers made a leaping catch on in front of five Lions defenders at the front of the end zone for a 27–23 victory.

"Until that clock ticks zero, there's no such thing as certain victory," Caldwell said after the game. "That's why I never smile during the course of games."

The Packers' Richard Rodgers catches a fourth-quarter touchdown to beat the Lions 27–23 at Ford Field.
COURTESY OF GETTY IMAGES

WHITEHEAD

Mercedes-Benz Superdome
LIONS
81

Calvin Johnson leaves the field following a game against the New Orleans Saints at the Mercedes-Benz Superdome on December 21, 2015 in New Orleans.
COURTESY OF GETTY IMAGES

MARCH 8, 2016

CALVIN CALLS IT QUITS

SEVENTEEN YEARS after Barry Sanders abruptly retired from the NFL, Calvin Johnson pulled a similar vanishing act that likewise left him temporarily at odds with the organization.

One of the greatest receivers in NFL history, Johnson announced his retirement March 8, 2016, at the age of 30 after nine star-studded seasons in Detroit. Unlike Sanders, Johnson told several close friends and people within the organization he was walking away immediately after the 2015 season, though he and the Lions waited to make it official until the start of free agency.

Johnson played through knee, ankle, and finger injuries in his final few seasons and had considered retirement the previous spring, but his father convinced him to stay another year after the Lions' 2014 playoff appearance. He played all 16 games in 2015 and caught 88 passes, the second most by any receiver in the final year of his career, but felt he could no longer perform to his high standard.

"Everybody wants to know why I retired, but it's more so, I put a lot into the game and it's taken a lot out of me and that's where I'm at right now," Johnson said in his first public comments months after his retirement.

Johnson, who acknowledged that the Lions' lack of success also contributed to his decision, finished his NFL career with 731 catches for 11,619 yards and 83 touchdowns. He led the league in receiving twice, was a member of the 2010 All-Decade team, and has the highest per-game receiving average (86.1 ypg) of anyone who has played at least five seasons in the NFL.

Johnson spent several years estranged from the organization after it forced him to repay $1.6 million of his signing bonus at the time of his retirement. The relationship softened after he entered the Hall of Fame in 2021, and Rod Wood said Johnson was "completely" back in the fold in 2024.

"He's the greatest football player, greatest receiver that I've ever played with—that I've ever seen before," running back Reggie Bush said in 2013. "I think that pretty much sums it up."

2016

FIVE-FINGER DISCOUNT

THE LIONS held their own without Calvin Johnson early in the 2016 season and reached mid-December in control of the NFC North. They beat the Bears in a Week 14 game to improve to 9–4—two games ahead of both the Packers and Vikings—but Matthew Stafford banged hands with Bears defender Leonard Floyd early in the game and dislocated the tip of the middle finger on his throwing hand.

The injury did not require surgery, but it limited Stafford the rest of the season and ultimately kept the Lions from winning their first division title in 23 years. Playing with an assortment of gloves, including one that covered his middle finger but left most of the rest of his hand exposed, Stafford threw five interceptions in the final 15 quarters of the regular season—the same as he had in the team's first 12 games.

The Lions lost December road tilts to the Giants and Cowboys and hosted Green Bay in the regular-season finale with the division on the line. For the second time in three years, they watched the Packers celebrate at their expense. Stafford completed 26 of 41 passes for 347 yards and two touchdowns, but he also threw an interception on the goal line and overthrew an open Golden Tate on a would-be touchdown in the game's second series.

Matthew Stafford flexes his finger after taking a hit during the second quarter of a game against the Chicago Bears at Ford Field on December 11, 2016. Stafford returned to the field wearing a glove on the injured hand.
COURTESY OF GETTY IMAGES

JANUARY 7, 2017

SELF-DESTRUCTION IN SEATTLE

DESPITE THEIR season-ending three-game losing streak, the Lions backed into the playoffs when the Giants beat Washington in Week 17. They drew the Seahawks as the six seed, then laid another egg in the postseason.

Matthew Stafford completed 18 of 32 passes for a modest 205 yards, but the Lions were their own worst enemies in a 26–6 loss. They dropped four passes, committed four personal fouls, and let Michigan native Thomas Rawls, who averaged 38.8 yards rushing in the nine regular-season games he played, run for 161 yards and a touchdown on 27 carries.

Jim Caldwell called the Lions' performance "inexplicable," while Stafford fell to 0–3 in the playoffs.

"This is like every other professional league," Stafford said. "It's a make-plays-or-don't-make-plays league and we didn't make them."

The Lions did not beat a team that made the playoffs all season and lost their final four games by a combined 59 points. Despite persistent questions about Caldwell's job security, Bob Quinn, who missed out on the window to interview coaching candidates on teams with a playoff bye for the second straight season—including his old team, the Patriots—opted to bring his head coach back for another year.

The Lions couldn't stop the Seahawks' Thomas Rawls in their January 2017 playoff matchup.
COURTESY OF GETTY IMAGES

SEPTEMBER 24, 2017

LOSING LIKE CLOCKWORK

FROM PICKED-UP penalty flags to process-of-the-catch rules, the Lions have found plenty of cruel and unusual ways to lose games over the years. Another example was on September 24, 2017, when they lost to the Atlanta Falcons, 30–26, on an obscure 10-second clock runoff.

With 12 seconds to play, Matthew Stafford completed a short pass to Golden Tate on third-and-goal from the Atlanta 1-yard line for what appeared to be the winning touchdown.

Officials ruled Tate caught the ball and crossed the goal line with 8 seconds on the clock, but the call was overturned on replay when video showed Falcons safety Brian Poole touched Tate on the back of his shoulder as Tate's knee hit the ground with the ball inches short of the end zone.

Because the play would have resulted in a live-clock situation and the Lions were out of timeouts, officials enforced a 10-second runoff, ending the game to the astonishment of players and the Ford Field crowd.

Caldwell said both the replay decision and clock runoff were correct, but that didn't take the sting out of a loss the Lions felt they did not deserve.

"I didn't personally find out about the 10-second runoff until I was actually speaking to the referees and then they brought it to my knowledge," Tate told WJBK-TV Fox 2 after the game. "Tough, man. It's a tough way to lose."

Golden Tate catches the ball as Brian Poole of the Atlanta Falcons touches him and his knee hits the ground.
COURTESY OF GETTY IMAGES

THE PATRIOT WAY AND THE PENCIL

THE LIONS were eliminated from playoff contention with a sloppy loss to the Bengals on Christmas Eve 2017, and Bob Quinn fired Jim Caldwell a week later and hired his former colleague with the Patriots and the coach he had long yearned to bring to Detroit, Matt Patricia, as his replacement.

Quinn and Patricia shared a roster-building philosophy and taste for players, but their union got off to a rocky start when, three months after he was hired, news surfaced that Patricia had been charged with sexual assault as a college student on spring break in Texas. The case never went to trial and Patricia denied wrongdoing, but the allegations were new to Quinn and the Lions and cast a pall over the rest of Patricia's tenure in Detroit.

By the end of his first training camp, Patricia, who always kept a pencil behind his ear, had alienated much of the Lions locker room with his authoritarian ways and inauthentic personality. He sometimes showed up late to his own meetings, and players felt he was demeaning to them and what they accomplished under Caldwell.

On the field, the Lions got off to a fast start under Patricia when Quandre Diggs intercepted a Sam Darnold pass and returned it for a touchdown on the first scrimmage play of Patricia's first game against the New York Jets. But that game, like the rest of his tenure, spiraled quickly out of control.

The Lions lost that 2018 opener 48–17 and went 6–10 in Patricia's first season as coach. Diggs, one of the locker-room leaders, was traded a year later; Pro Bowl cornerback Darius Slay was shipped out of town not long after that; and the Lions got progressively worse defensively under Patricia, whose calling card as an assistant was on that side of the ball with the Patriots, where he won three Super Bowls.

On November 27, 2020, a day after a Thanksgiving loss to the Texans, the Lions fired Quinn and Patricia, who went 13–29–1 in their time together in Detroit.

Head coach Matt Patricia walks to the locker room at halftime during a game against the New York Jets. New York defeated the Lions 48–17.
COURTESY OF GETTY IMAGES

JANUARY 21, 2021

"WE'RE GOING TO BITE A KNEECAP OFF"

THE PATRIOT WAY was a disaster in Detroit, so when the Lions set out to replace Bob Quinn and Matt Patricia, they did things differently.

In parallel searches run by Sheila Ford Hamp, Rod Wood, Chris Spielman, and Mike Disner, the Lions hired Saints assistant head coach Dan Campbell and Rams director of college scouting Brad Holmes as coach and GM. The two had never met before taking the jobs, but they shared similar visions of culture and collaboration.

Holmes, a draft savant who helped build the Rams into Super Bowl contenders, was introduced first, followed by Campbell, a tight end with the Lions from 2006–2008, a few days later.

Wood said the search committee "did this process better than we did the last process" and promised "it's going to result in a better result." And Campbell, roundly praised for his genuineness and leadership ability, delivered one of the most colorful introductory news conferences in NFL history.

"We're going to kick you in the teeth," Campbell said. "And when you punch us back, we're going to smile at you and when you knock us down, we're going to get up, and on the way up, we're going to bite a kneecap off. And we're going to stand up and then it's going to take two more shots to knock us down. And on the way up, we're going to take your other kneecap, and we're going to get up and then it's going to take three shots to get us down. And when we do, we're going to take another hunk out of you. Before long, we're . . . going to be the last one standing."

Campbell's words raised eyebrows across the NFL, but resonated powerfully in Detroit.

Lions general manager Brad Holmes (left) and head coach Dan Campbell talk after a Lions training camp practice in 2021.
COURTESY OF GETTY IMAGES

JANUARY 30, 2021

THE TRADE THAT CHANGED THE FRANCHISE

MATTHEW STAFFORD had grown tired of losing after 12 not-quite-good-enough seasons in Detroit. He did not want to go through another rebuild. And after the 2020 season, he sat down with Rod Wood and, with Sheila Ford Hamp on speakerphone, asked for a trade.

Brad Holmes found out about Stafford's request shortly before he was offered the job, and his first task as Lions GM was to engineer a deal that would both make Stafford happy—after years of alienating its stars, the organization wanted to do right by Stafford—and fast-forward the franchise's rebuild.

By the end of January, seven or eight teams had shown interest in Stafford, with some more serious than others. Washington, with ex–Lions GM Martin Mayhew in charge, and the Carolina Panthers were among the suitors that offered 2021 first-round picks, but Holmes swung a deal with his old team the Rams that included two future first-round choices in 2022–23, a third-round pick in 2021, and veteran quarterback Jared Goff.

Holmes favored the extra draft capital over the certainty of Carolina's single top-10 choice, and he considered Goff, who was still in the prime of his career and in need of a change of scenery after falling out of favor with Rams coach Sean McVay, an important part of the deal.

The Lions spent the extra 2021 third-round pick on safety Ifeatu Melifonwu; used the Rams' 2022 first-rounder as part of a package to move up and draft receiver Jameson Williams; struck gold with the Rams' 2023 first-rounder at No. 6 overall, which they traded out of and used the picks they acquired to take running back Jahmyr Gibbs and tight end Sam LaPorta; and rebuilt Goff into a Pro Bowl quarterback.

Stafford won a Super Bowl in his first season in L.A., and the trade may have closed the book on Bobby Layne's curse, with the Lions granting one franchise quarterback and Highland Park High grad's request to be traded 63 years after their last championship cycle ended with the shocking deal of another.

Matthew Stafford waves to fans after a game against the Tampa Bay Buccaneers at Ford Field. The Lions won 34–17.
COURTESY OF GETTY IMAGES

APRIL 29, 2021

BUILDING A BEAST UP FRONT

BRAD HOLMES was a key part of the Rams' scouting staff that built one of the best defensive lines in football. They spent first-round picks on linemen Robert Quinn in 2011 and Michael Brockers in 2012, and two years later hit the mother lode when the Lions passed on Aaron Donald, leaving him there for the Rams to take with the 13th overall pick.

On the morning of his first draft as Lions GM, Holmes said he wanted to build a "beast" like that in Detroit. He didn't specify what position group he was talking about—but he didn't need to after the Lions took Oregon offensive tackle Penei Sewell at No. 7 overall.

The draft's best offensive line prospect even though he sat out the Covid season of 2020, Sewell joined a unit that already was considered one of the best in the NFL with Taylor Decker at left tackle, Frank Ragnow at center, and Jonah Jackson and Halapoulivaati Vaitai at guards.

Sewell started the first eight games of his rookie season at left tackle with Decker out with an injury, then moved to right tackle in the second half of the year. He made his first Pro Bowl in 2022 and was a first-team All-Pro in 2023, when at 23 years old he already was considered the best right tackle in the game.

The Lions' Frank Ragnow (77), Penei Sewell (58), and Taylor Decker (68) make up one of the best offensive lines in the NFL.
COURTESY OF GETTY IMAGES

MAY 1, 2021

AMON-RA ST. BROWN AND THE SWEET 16

PENEI SEWELL wasn't the only cornerstone player Brad Holmes landed in the 2021 draft. With the 112th overall pick early in the fourth round, the Lions took USC receiver Amon-Ra St. Brown.

Though a slow 40 time (4.61 seconds) held down his draft stock, St. Brown embodied the characteristics Holmes said "equate success to a wide receiver."

"He's instinctive, he's tough, he's got grit, he's savvy," Holmes said. "He's one of the most impressive blockers that I saw in this draft class. And I just think in that phase of the game, the tenacity that he brings in that phase just says a lot about his intangibles and his football character."

St. Brown led the Lions in receptions and receiving yards in each of his first three seasons and was a first-team All-Pro in 2023, when he set career highs with 119 catches, 1,515 yards, and 10 touchdowns.

His production has far exceeded his draft position thanks to an insatiable work ethic—he catches 202 balls off a Jugs machine every day after practice—and the sizable chip he still carries on his shoulder as a Day 3 draft pick. St. Brown keeps a notebook with a list of his goals for every season and the names of the 16 receivers drafted before him that he said in 2023 he still refers to every day.

"It's something I'll never forget," he told NFL Network. "Something I make sure I'm always reminded of."

Amon-Ra St. Brown celebrating after a touchdown. COURTESY OF GETTY IMAGES

MEKARI
65
85
RAVENS

SEPTEMBER 26, 2021

ANOTHER KICK IN THE GUT

THE LIONS stumbled out of the gate in Dan Campbell's first season as coach, starting a league-worst 0–10–1. Four of those losses came by a field goal or less, three on the final play of the game, and one in particularly gut-wrenching fashion when Justin Tucker made an NFL-record 66-yard field goal off the crossbar to give the Ravens a 19–17 victory in Week 3.

The Lions rallied from a 13–0 second-half deficit to take a 17-16 lead with 1:04 to play. They sacked Baltimore quarterback Lamar Jackson twice on the ensuing series, leaving the Ravens in an impossible fourth-and-19 from their own 16-yard line with 26 seconds left, then watched Jackson complete a 36-yard pass to Sammy Watkins to get the Ravens to the edge of field-goal range.

After a spike to stop the clock and another quick incompletion, the second coming when the ball was snapped after the play clock appeared to expire, the Ravens sent Tucker out for a 66-yard kick. The ball hit the crossbar, bounced straight up in the air and tumbled just over as Ravens players stormed the field in celebration.

"About as big a gut punch as I've ever been a part of," Jared Goff said after the game. "They made a field goal by a foot. He made a great kick. Your hat's off to him."

Ravens kicker Justin Tucker beats the Lions with a record-setting 66-yard field goal.
COURTESY OF GETTY IMAGES

ATL
ATL

APRIL 28, 2022

AIDAN HUTCHINSON STAYS HOME

THE LIONS won three of their final six games in 2021 to salvage a 3-13-1 record. The victories were much-needed but cost them the No. 1 pick in a draft where the prize seemed to be Michigan defensive end Aidan Hutchinson.

Hutchinson was a polished and productive college pass rusher whose high motor and three-down ability were attractive to teams. But when the Jacksonville Jaguars opted for upside and took Georgia defensive end Travon Walker No. 1 overall, the Lions turned their draft card in for Hutchinson so fast they were admonished by the league.

"We deserve this player, we do, and this player deserves us also as a coaching staff," Lions defensive coordinator Aaron Glenn said. "This is a good time for Detroit."

Hutchinson, who grew up in Plymouth, Michigan, a short drive from Ford Field, had three sacks in his second career game and finished a standout rookie season with 9.5 sacks, three interceptions, and two fumble recoveries. He finished second in Defensive Rookie of the Year voting—Walker did not receive a vote—and followed that up with an 11.5-sack Pro Bowl campaign in 2023.

Just five Lions—Robert Porcher, Doug English, William Gay, Ziggy Ansah, and Mike Cofer—have had more sacks in a season since the stat became official in 1982.

Aidan Hutchinson sacks Desmond Ridder of the Atlanta Falcons.
COURTESY OF GETTY IMAGES

JANUARY 8, 2023

THE SPRINGBOARD TO SUCCESS

THE LIONS started slowly again in 2022, losing six of their first seven games. Sheila Ford Hamp felt compelled to give Dan Campbell a public vote of confidence in late October, and the team's fortunes turned shortly thereafter.

The Lions intercepted three Aaron Rodgers passes in a November win over the Packers, then beat the Bears a week later on a late Jamaal Williams touchdown. By the time Week 18 rolled around, the Lions were 8–8 and headed to Lambeau Field as the hottest team in football.

With nothing but pride to play for after they were eliminated from playoff contention shortly before kickoff, the Lions beat the Packers 20–16 to sweep the season series and knock Green Bay out of the playoffs. Jared Goff threw for 224 yards, Williams ran for two touchdowns, and Kerby Joseph intercepted Rodgers with 3:27 to play on what would be Rodgers's final pass as a Packer.

The Lions finished the season on an 8–2 tear that put the NFL on notice they would be a team to reckon with in 2023.

"It was more than just ruining their season, it was showing the world who we are," Amon-Ra St. Brown said. "To be on Sunday night for the first time all year, in Green Bay, with playoff implications on the line for them, we just wanted to go out there and we wanted to show everyone we want some respect here in Detroit."

Jamaal Williams rushes for a touchdown in the last game of the 2022 season.
COURTESY OF GETTY IMAGES

Josh Paschal (93), Alim McNeill (54), and Derrick Barnes (55) celebrate a big third-down stop against the Kansas City Chiefs.
COURTESY OF GETTY IMAGES

2023

A MAGICAL REGULAR-SEASON RIDE

WITH DAN CAMPBELL as the face of the franchise, one of the league's most creative offenses under coordinator Ben Johnson, and a young defensive nucleus led by Aidan Hutchinson, the Lions entered 2023 as overwhelming favorites to win the NFC North.

The NFL scheduled the Lions for its Thursday-night season opener, and when they upset the defending Super Bowl champion Chiefs 21–20 at Arrowhead Stadium, it only raised expectations more.

The Lions started 5–1, won four straight games by double-digits, and were accompanied at most road games by tens of thousands of fans clad in Honolulu blue and silver. They led the North wire-to-wire and clinched their first division title in 30 years with a 30–24 win over the Vikings on Christmas Eve.

"This has been a long time coming," Campbell said after the game. "And look, I'm proud of all the Lions fans out there that have been dying for this for years, man. That was for you, too. I know it's been a long time. You deserve that. And it's not over. That's just one."

The Lions had a chance to earn the NFC's No. 1 seed with two games to play, but lost a controversial Week 17 game at Dallas when officials incorrectly administered a tackle-eligible play on a two-point conversion. They finished 12–5, tied for the most wins in franchise history, and entered the playoffs as the three seed in the NFC.

JANUARY 14, 2024

"ABSOLUTELY ELECTRIC": THE PLAYOFFS COME TO FORD FIELD

THE LIONS hosted the Rams in their first home playoff game in 30 years on January 14, 2024, and the football gods couldn't have created a more perfect matchup.

Matthew Stafford was playing his first game at Ford Field since he asked for a trade, against the team he never could lead to playoff success. Jared Goff was facing his old team with a chance to show up the coach who ran him out of town. And a sellout crowd of 66,367, the eighth largest in Ford Field history, packed the stadium an hour early and partied long into the night.

"That was absolutely electric," Dan Campbell said after the game. "I was coming down for pregame warm-up and you could just feel it. It was humming. The building was humming, and I swear you could feel the electricity down the tunnel from where I was coming down, and it only just grew from there."

Lions fans mercilessly booed Stafford, their one-time hero, and serenaded Goff repeatedly with chants of, "Jar-ed Goff, Jar-ed Goff."

Both quarterbacks played masterful games, with Stafford throwing for 367 yards and two touchdowns and Goff going for 277 yards and one score and staking the Lions to a 24–23 lead with 7 minutes to play. The Rams drove into field goal range on their final possession, but McVay opted to punt after Stafford threw incomplete on third-and-14 following a holding penalty that backed them up to the 44-yard line.

The Lions picked up two first downs on the ensuing possession, and the Rams were helpless to stop the clock in the final minute after burning two timeouts early in the second half to avoid delay-of-game penalties because of the noisy crowd.

"That's the best home atmosphere I've ever played in front of," Goff said. "It's a special place to play and I've only been here for three years, but to see us come from where we were to where we are now and the fans endure some of that, it's special to be able to get this W for them and for this group in our locker room."

Matthew Stafford of the Los Angeles Rams hugs Jared Goff following the Lions' victory in the NFC wild-card playoff game at Ford Field.
COURTESY OF GETTY IMAGES

JANUARY 21, 2024

LIONS ADVANCE TO NFC CHAMPIONSHIP GAME

THREE YEARS to the day of his memorable kneecaps speech, Dan Campbell delivered something better to Detroit—a spot in the NFC championship game.

The Lions beat the Buccaneers 31–23 in the divisional round of the playoffs January 21, 2024, in front of another raucous crowd at Ford Field. Jahmyr Gibbs and Amon-Ra St. Brown scored touchdowns on back-to-back possessions in the fourth quarter to break open a tie game, and Derrick Barnes intercepted a Baker Mayfield pass with 1:33 left to seal the victory.

Campbell became the first Lions coach to win two playoff games in the same season since George Wilson in 1957, and the Lions advanced to the NFC championship game for the second time in franchise history.

Asked after the game how the Lions compared to his vision for the team three years earlier when he was introduced as head coach, Campbell said he believed then "we would have a chance to compete with the big boys, and that's where we're at."

A week later, the Lions would face the 49ers in San Francisco with a trip to the Super Bowl on the line.

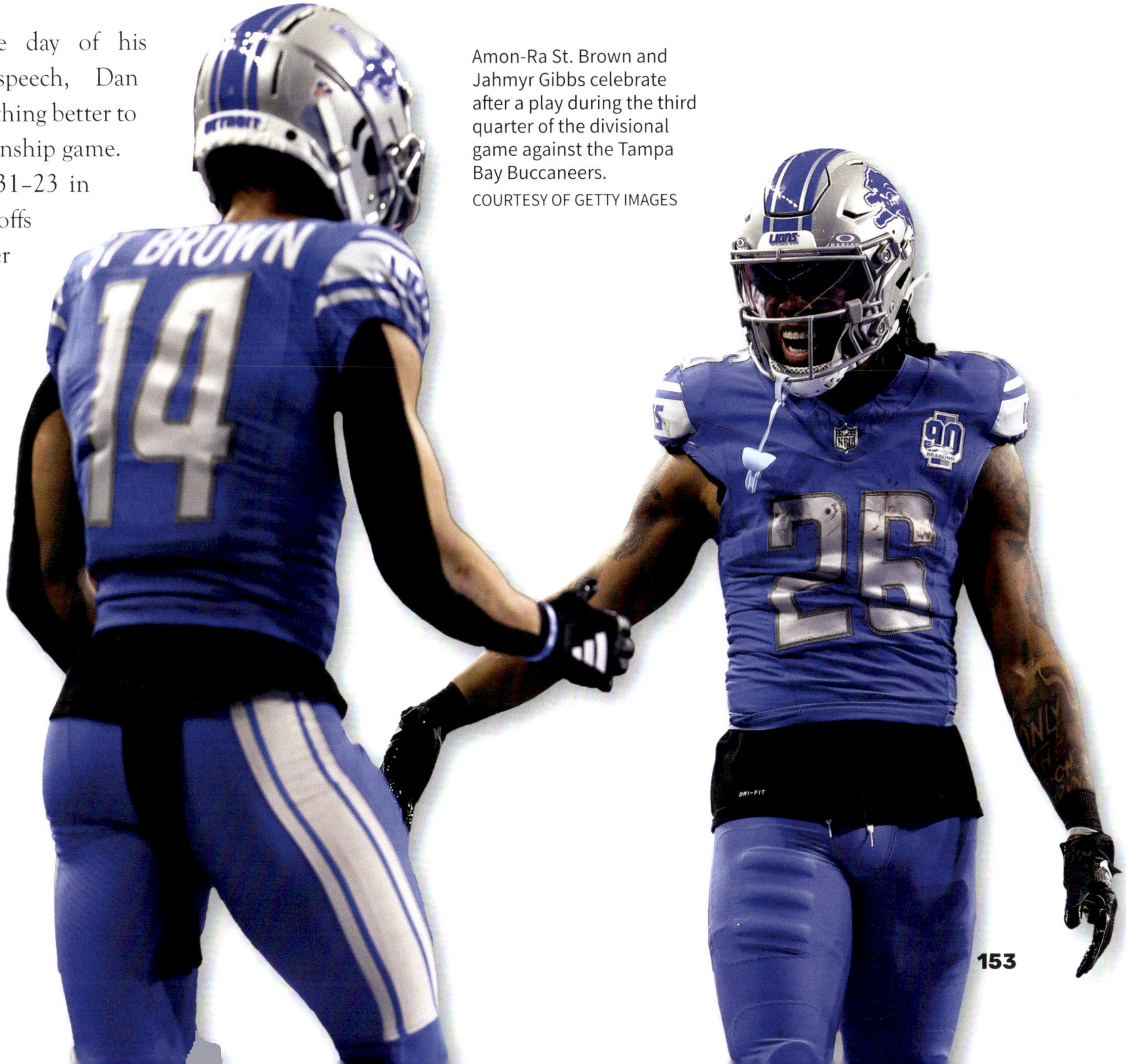

Amon-Ra St. Brown and Jahmyr Gibbs celebrate after a play during the third quarter of the divisional game against the Tampa Bay Buccaneers.
COURTESY OF GETTY IMAGES

JANUARY 28, 2024

A CRUSHING SECOND-HALF COLLAPSE

PLAYING 37 MILES from the site of their last road playoff win in 1957, the Lions played their best 30 minutes of football all year in the first half of the NFC championship game.

Jahmyr Gibbs, David Montgomery, and Jameson Williams scored rushing touchdowns, and when the Lions took a 24–7 lead into the locker room—the same score they trailed by at halftime of the 1957 Western Division final—they seemed destined to make their first-ever Super Bowl.

But things unraveled quickly in the second half. Gibbs fumbled. Josh Reynolds dropped two key passes. Dan Campbell passed on two long field goal tries to attempt fourth downs the Lions failed to convert. Kindle Vildor had a potential interception bounce off his facemask and into the arms of receiver Brandon Aiyuk for a long gain.

The 49ers scored 27 unanswered points, and the Lions managed only a late touchdown in a crushing 34–31 defeat.

"It's hard when you lose that way," an emotional Campbell said after the game. "You feel like you get your heart ripped out. So, but I'm proud of that group and I'll go anywhere with that group."

Two months later, Campbell seemed reenergized. He rewatched the second half of that game with his assistants and vowed the Lions would be "battle-hardened and ready to go" in 2024.

"We got to get over that hill and we can do it," he said. "And I love that we've got something to shoot for."

The Lions' magical 2023 season ended with a loss to Brock Purdy (13) and the San Francisco 49ers in the NFC championship game.
COURTESY OF GETTY IMAGES

Jared Goff leads a huddle prior to the NFC championship game against the San Francisco 49ers.
COURTESY OF GETTY IMAGES

INDEX

INDEX

Herman Moore celebrates a touchdown with teammates in the Lions' 1998 Thanksgiving win over the Pittsburgh Steelers.
COURTESY OF THE DETROIT LIONS

Running back Billy Sims scores on a 1-yard touchdown run during the Lions' 24–17 victory over the San Francisco 49ers on September 6, 1981, at the Pontiac Silverdome.
COURTESY OF GETTY IMAGES

INDEX

Fans hang a banner celebrating Barry Sanders at the Pontiac Silverdome.
COURTESY OF THE DETROIT LIONS